BEAUTIFUL BIRD PHOTOGRAPHY

A CURATED COLLECTION OF INTERNATIONAL PHOTOGRAPHERS

BY
CAROL GRAHAM

THANKS TO THE PHOTOGRAPHERS IN THIS BOOK

Aaliya Wahab, Ahmed Badawy, Alice Washington, Andreas Dress, Andrew Pons, Cindy Holmes, Andy Makely, Bill Mackie, Boris Smokrovic, Bradley Feller, Brandon Griggs, Chinh Le Duc, Chris Charles, Chris Smith, Dahiana Waszaj, Damon Hall, Deb Dowd, Deepak Nautiyal, Delaney Van, Dieny Portinanni, Domonik Lange, Greorie Berand, Hans Veth, James Lee, James Newcombe, J Dean, Jeremy Hynes, Johnathan Ciarocca, John McMahon, Luca Ambrosi, Lukasz Rawa, Madiba de African Inspiration, Mark Olsen, Mateusz, Mingjun Liu, Mohamed Elsayed, Naser Tamimi, Oliver Guillard, Patrice Bouchard, Peter Scholten, Photo by Beks, Ravin Rau, Ray Hennessy, Richard Lee, Ricardo Frantz, Rogean James Caleffi, Seiji Seiji, Shaira Torlao, Simon Berger, Sreenivas, Thomas Maximillian Lener, Yoksel Zok,Tomas Vydrzal.

Seiji Seiji (Cover Page)

More of their photo works on additional subjects can be found at Unsplash.com (a Division of Getty Images).

Many of the photographers whose works are displayed in this book are available for hire.

Their contact information can be found on their individual Unsplash pages or contact us at **photobookpublishers@gmail.com** and we will be happy to help you connect with them for your next project.

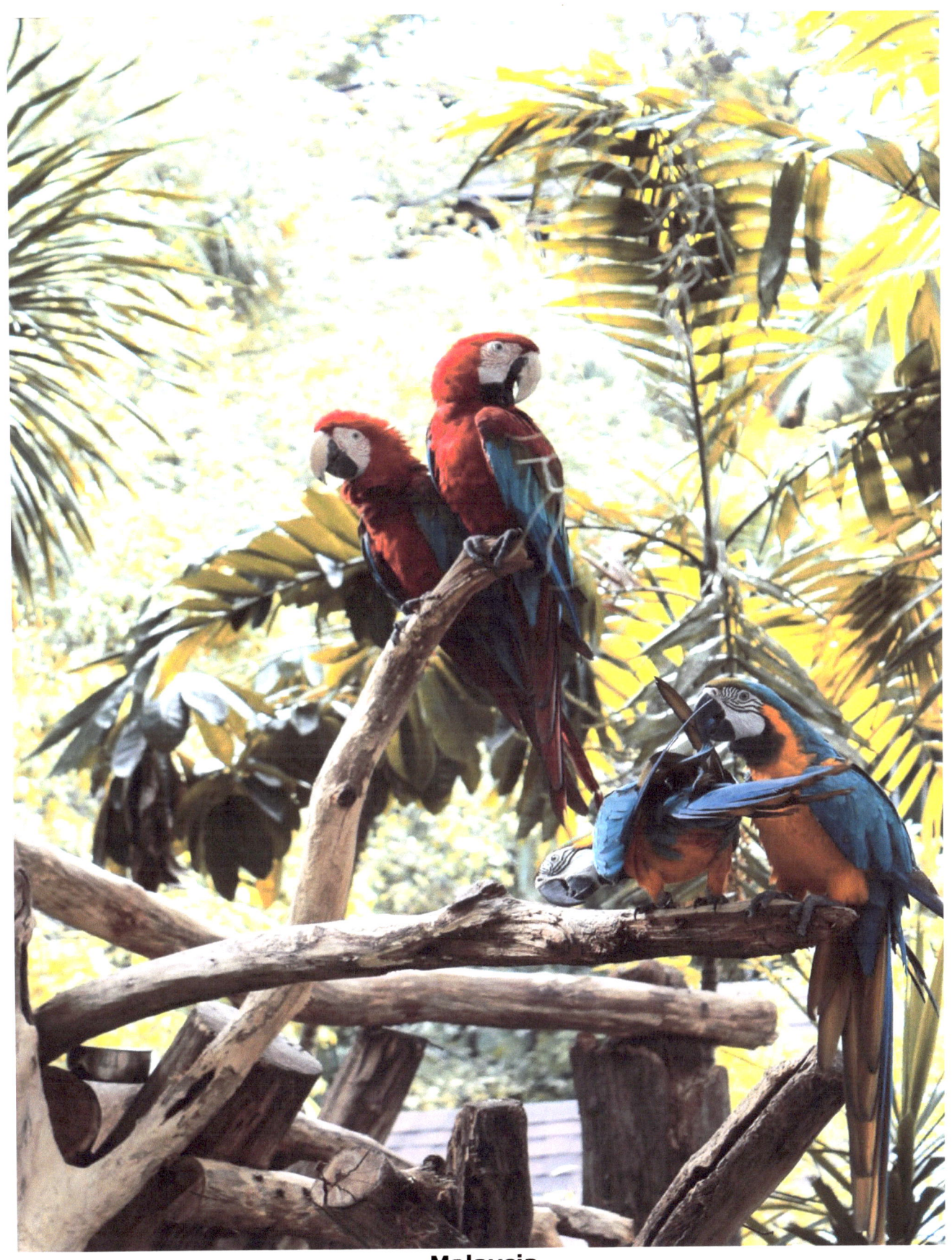

Malaysia
Photographer: Aaliya Wahab

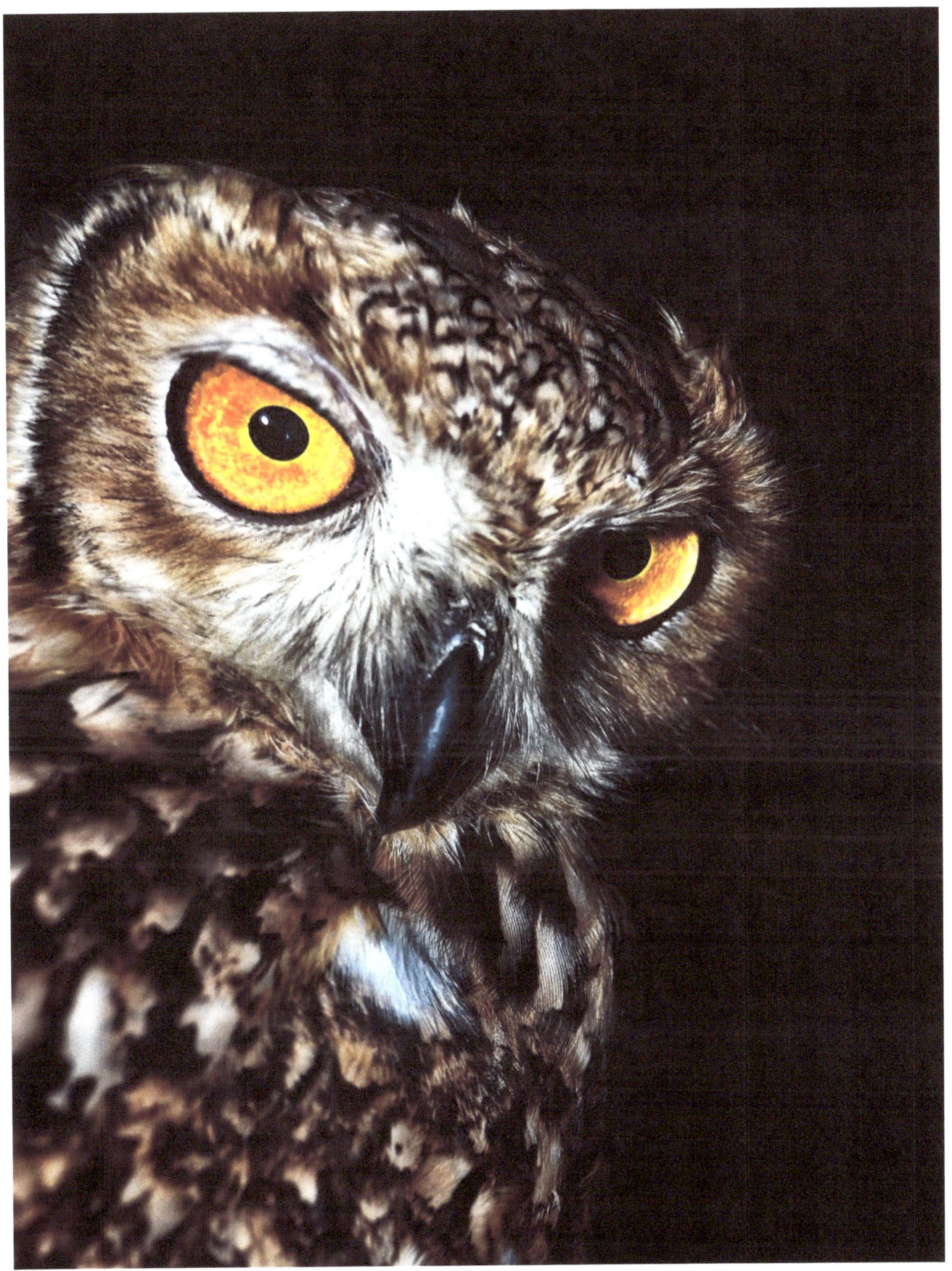

Alexandria, Egypt
Photographer: Ahmed Badawy – Alexandria, Egypt

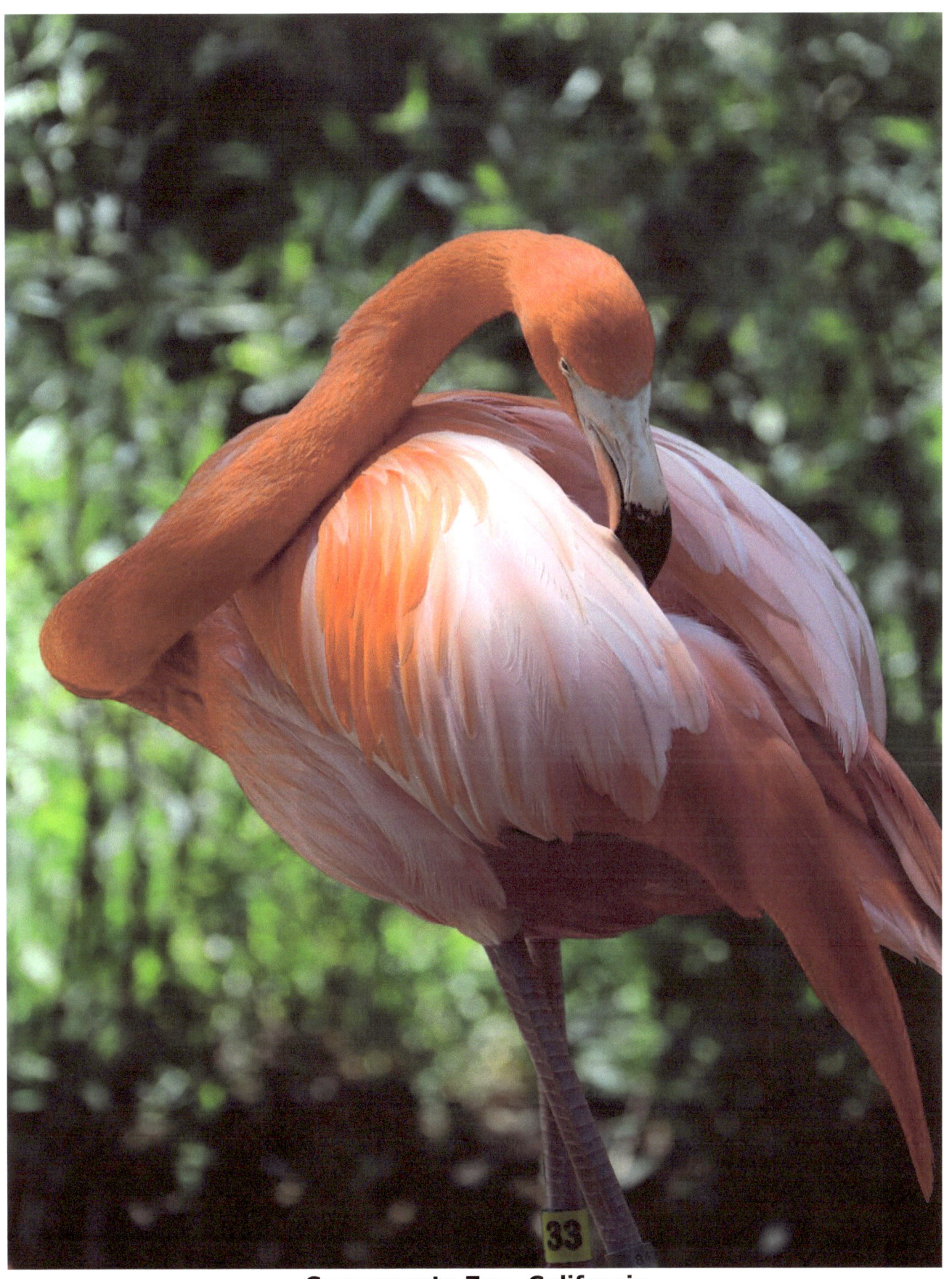

Sacramento Zoo, California
Photographer: Alice Washington

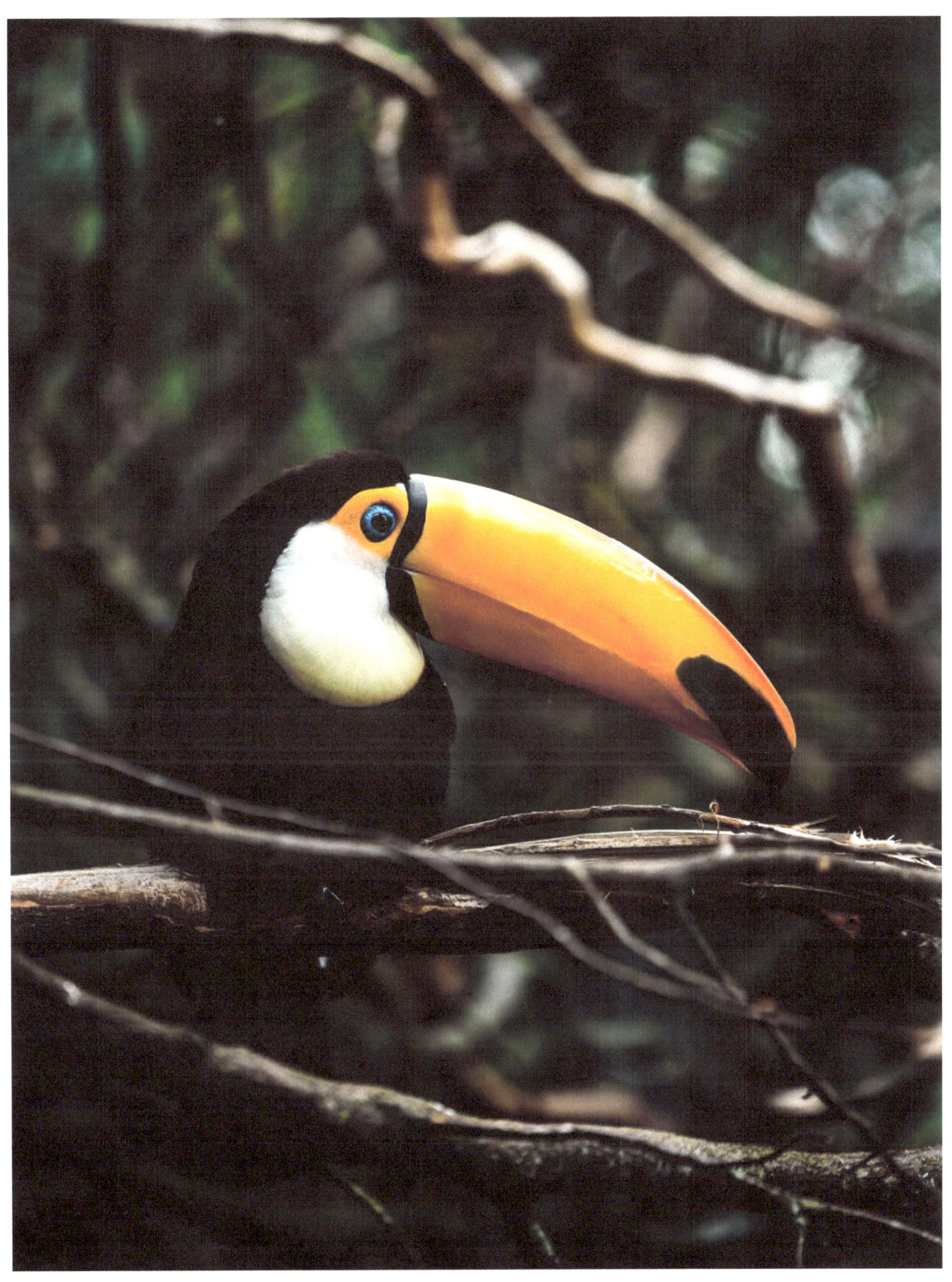

Photographer: Andreas Dress – Copenhagen, Denmark

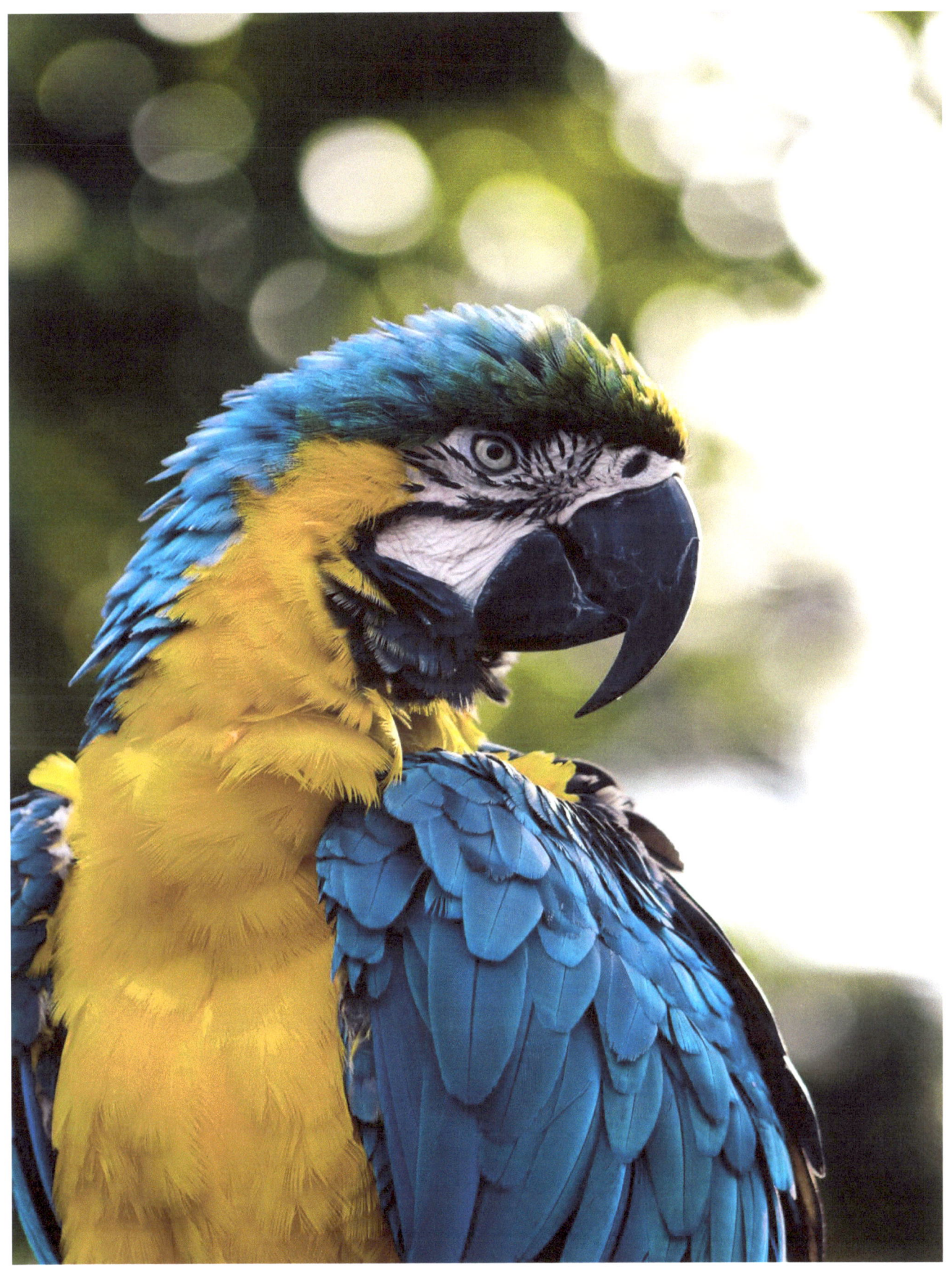

West Palm Beach, Florida
Photographer: Andrew Pons – Charlotte, North Carolina

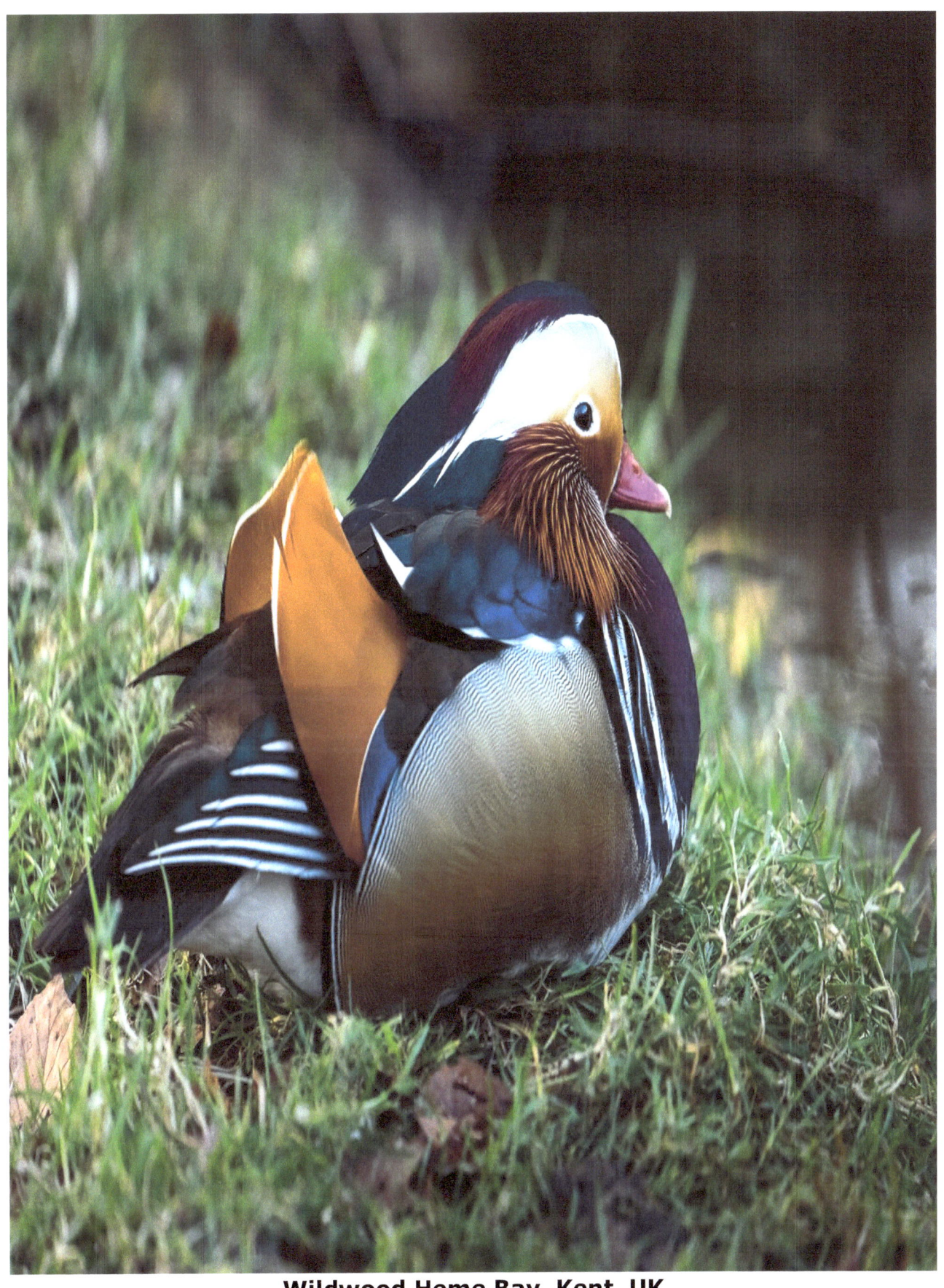

Wildwood Heme Bay, Kent, UK
Photographer: Andy Holmes – Chatham, Kent, UK

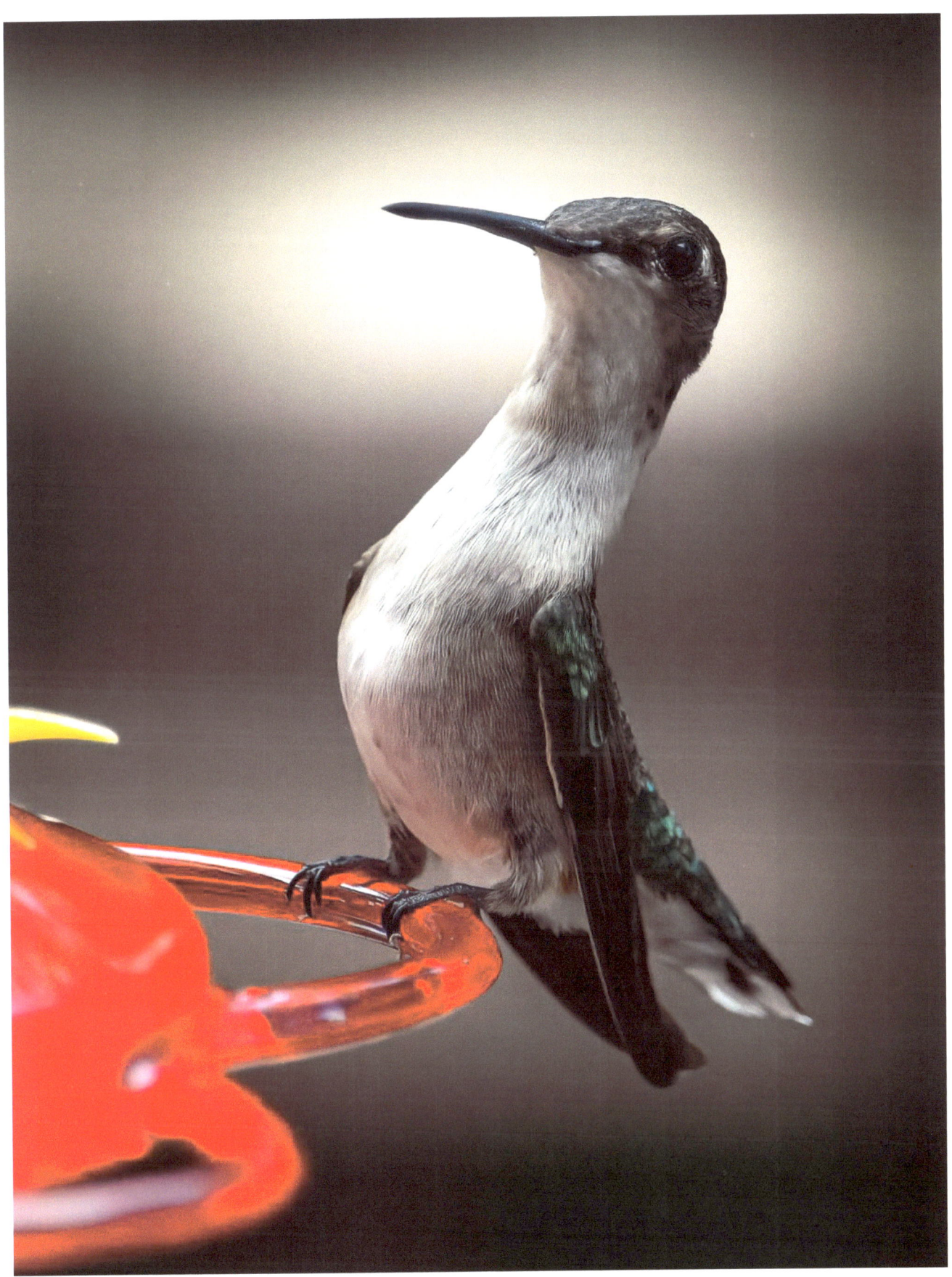

Photographer: Andy Makely

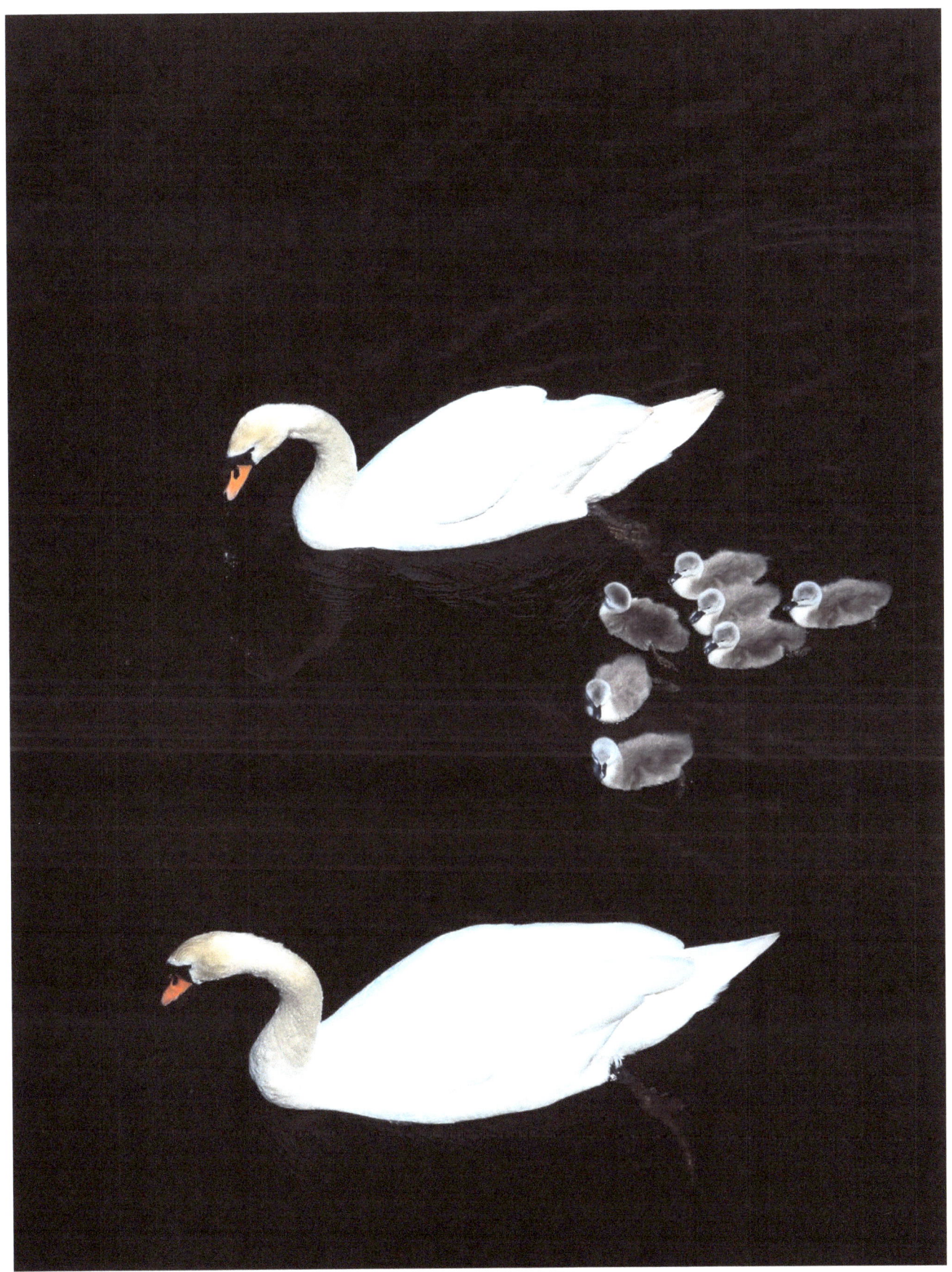

Eyemouth, UK
Photographer: Bill Mackie - Scotland

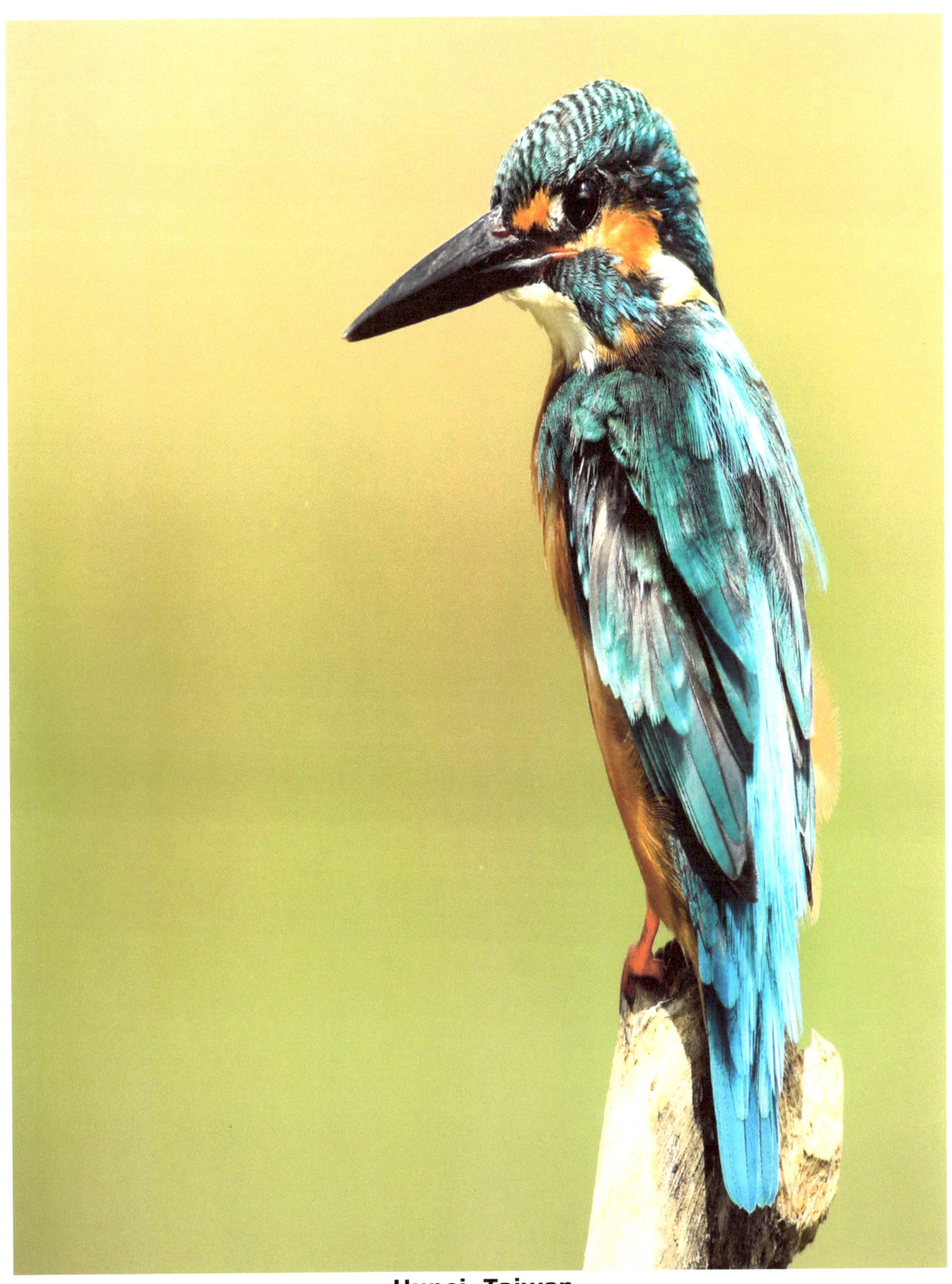

Hunei, Taiwan
Photographer: Boris Smokrovic, Taiwan

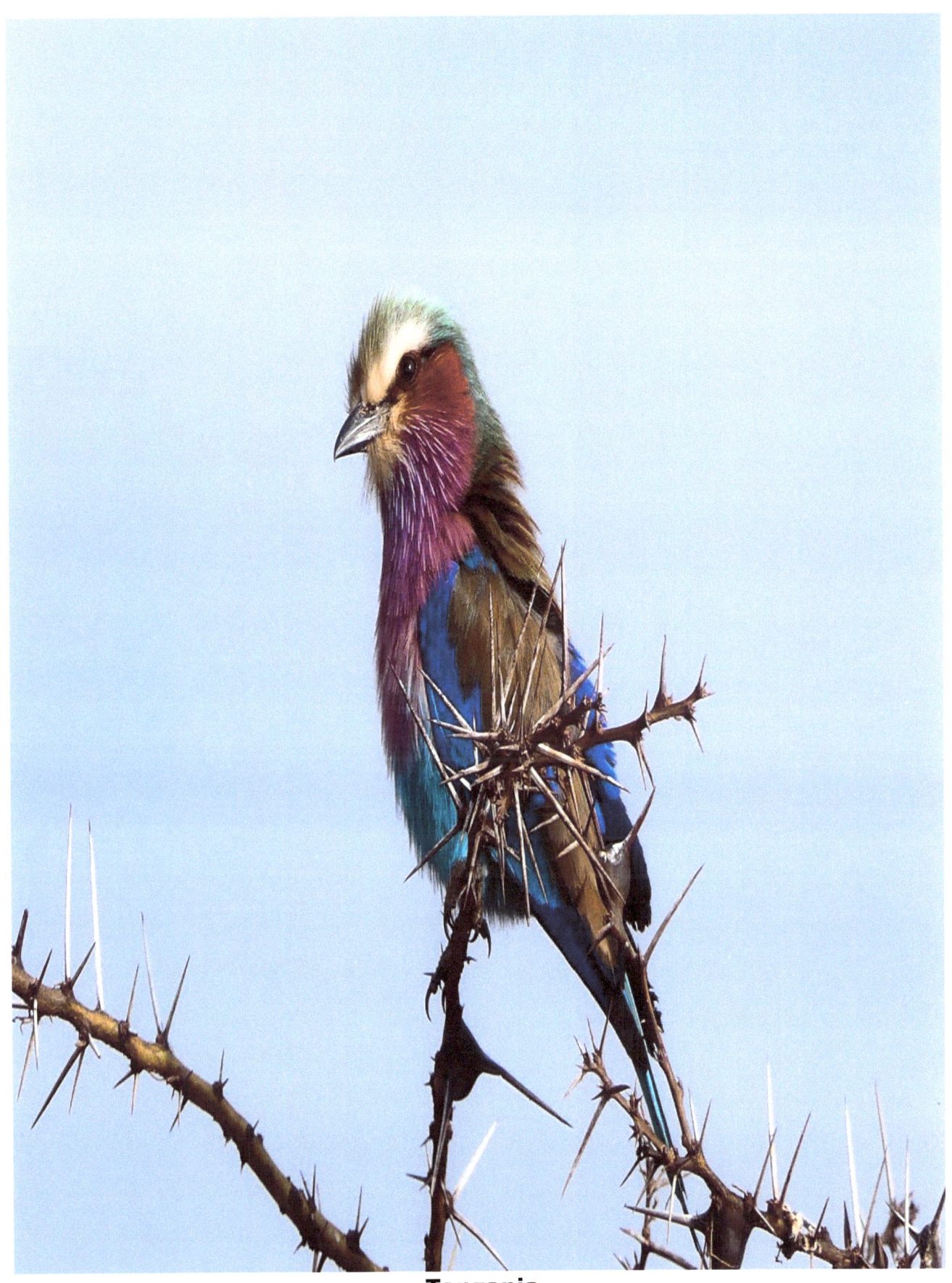

Tanzania
Photographer: Bradley Feller

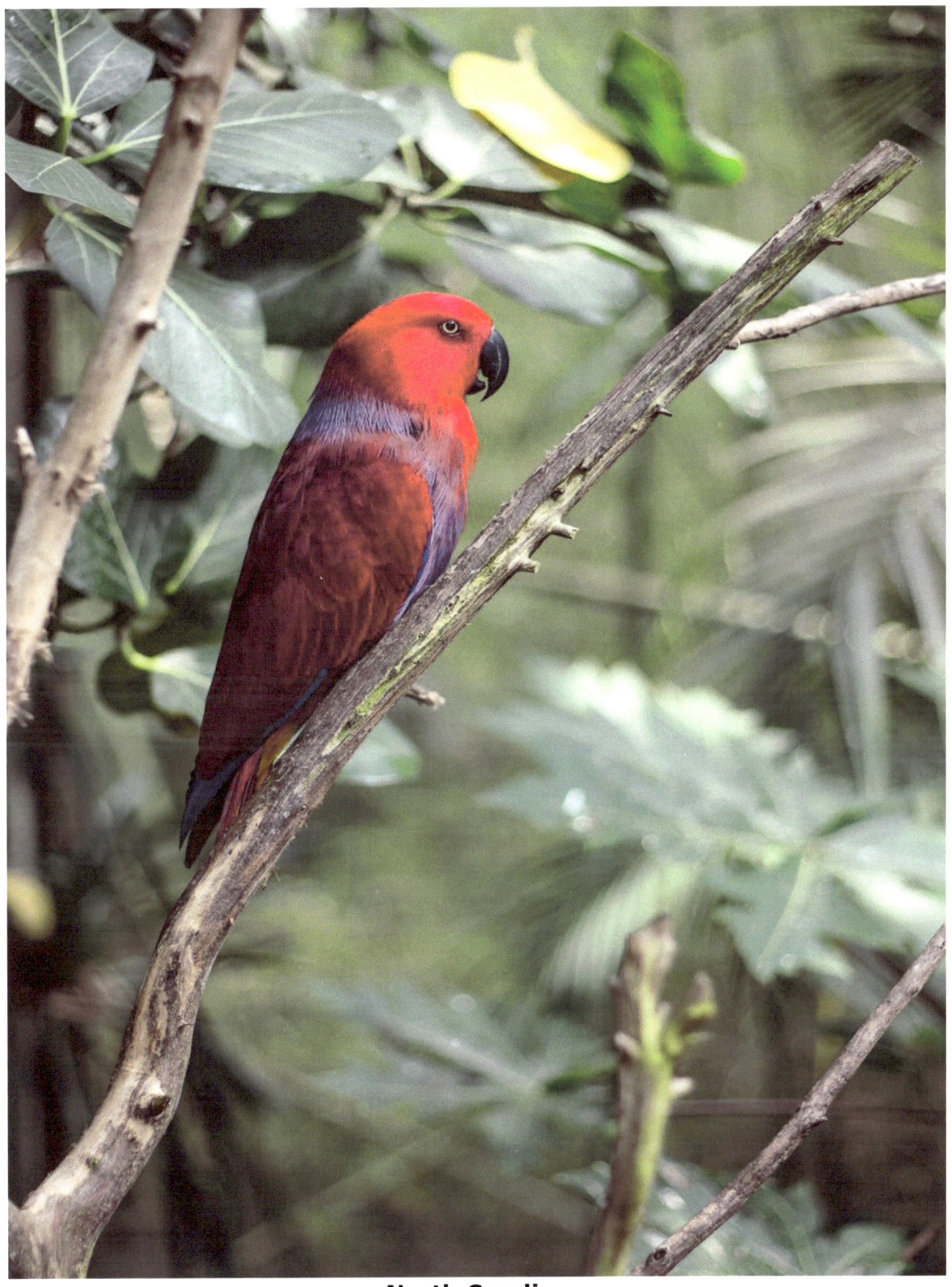

North Carolina
Photographer: Brandon Griggs – Raleigh, North Carolina

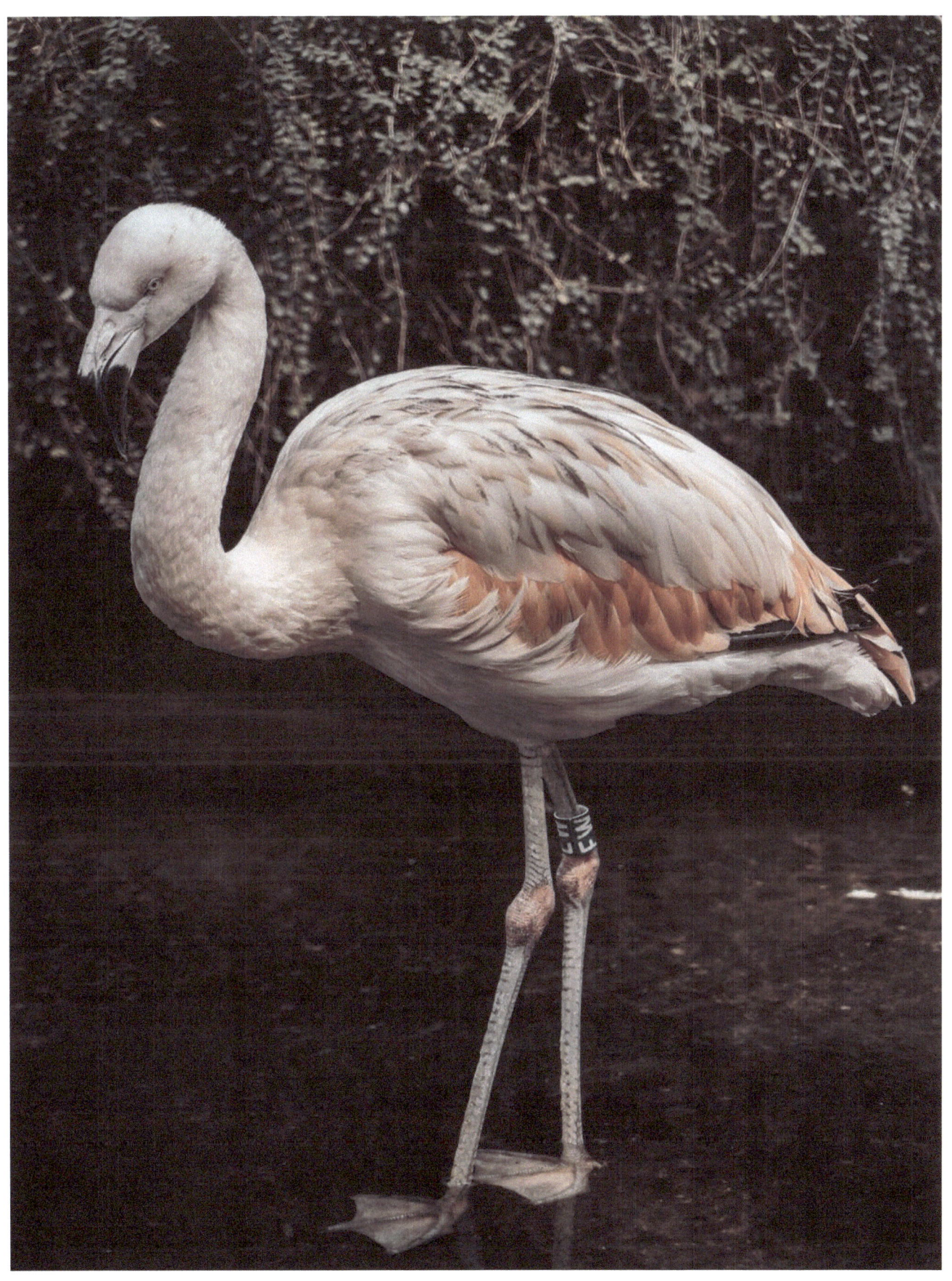

Photographer: Chinh Le Duc - Vietnam

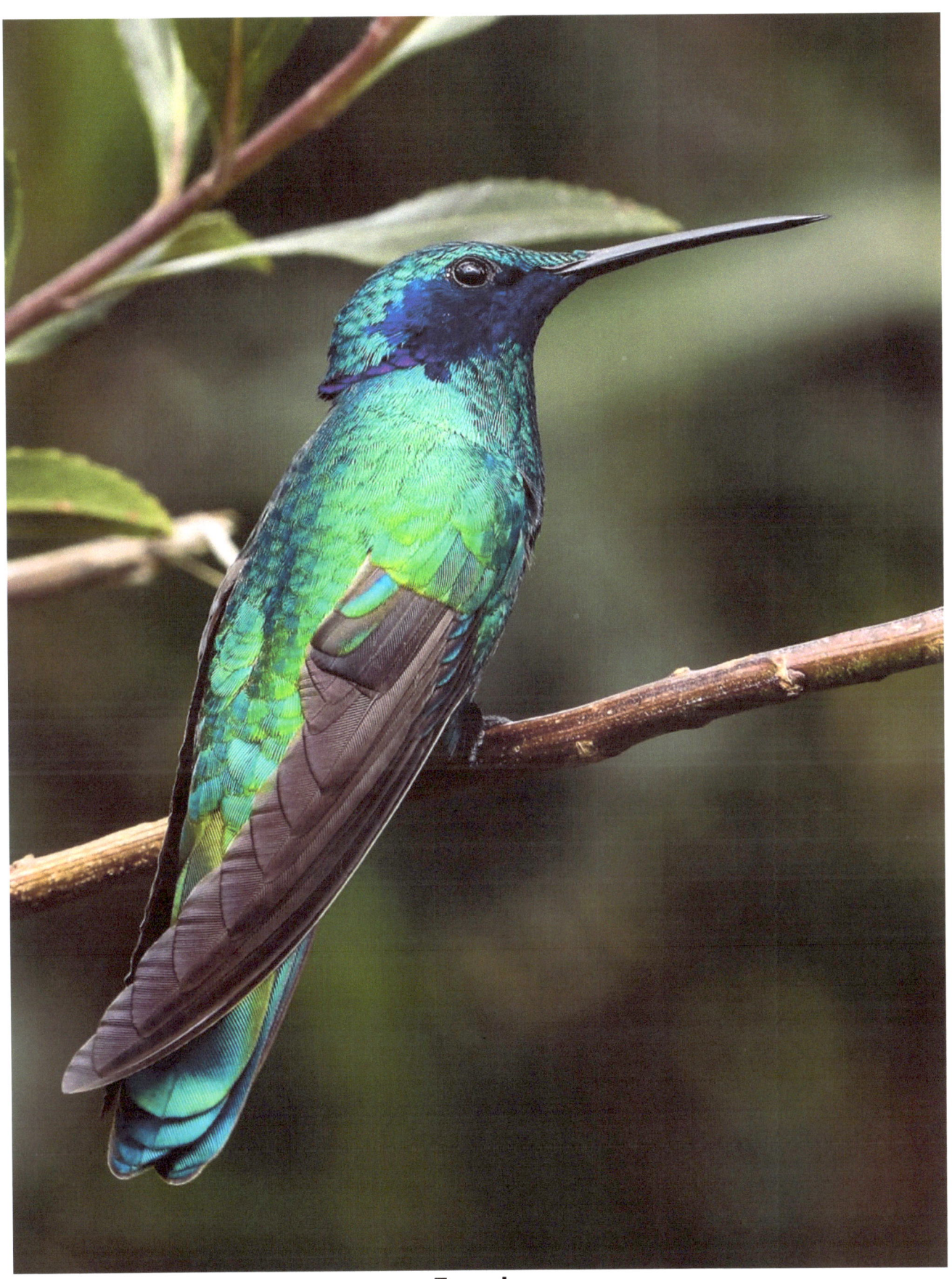

Ecuador
Photographer: Chris Charles – Sydney, Australia

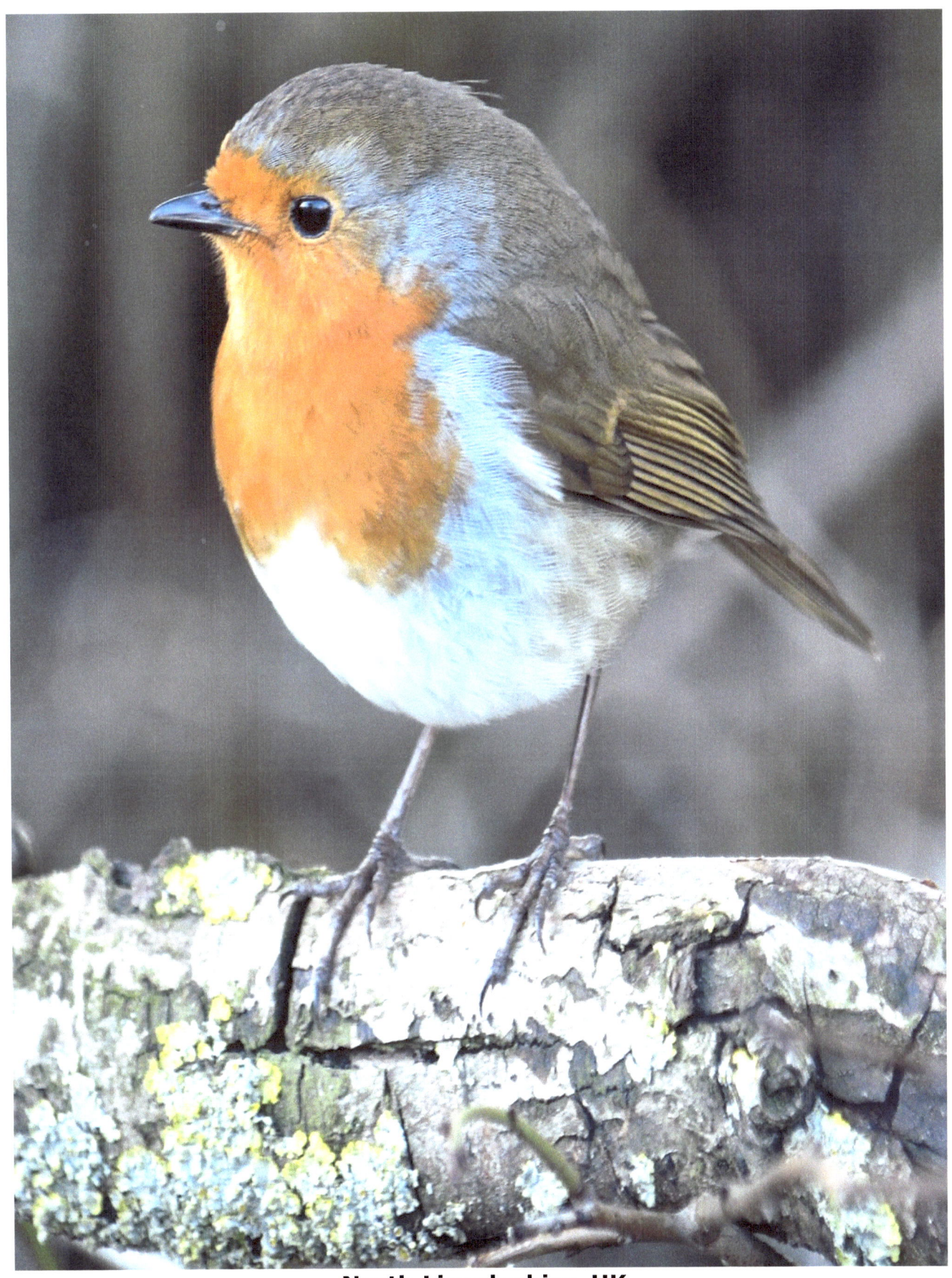

North Lincolnshire, UK
Photographer: Chris Smith, North Lincolnshire, UK

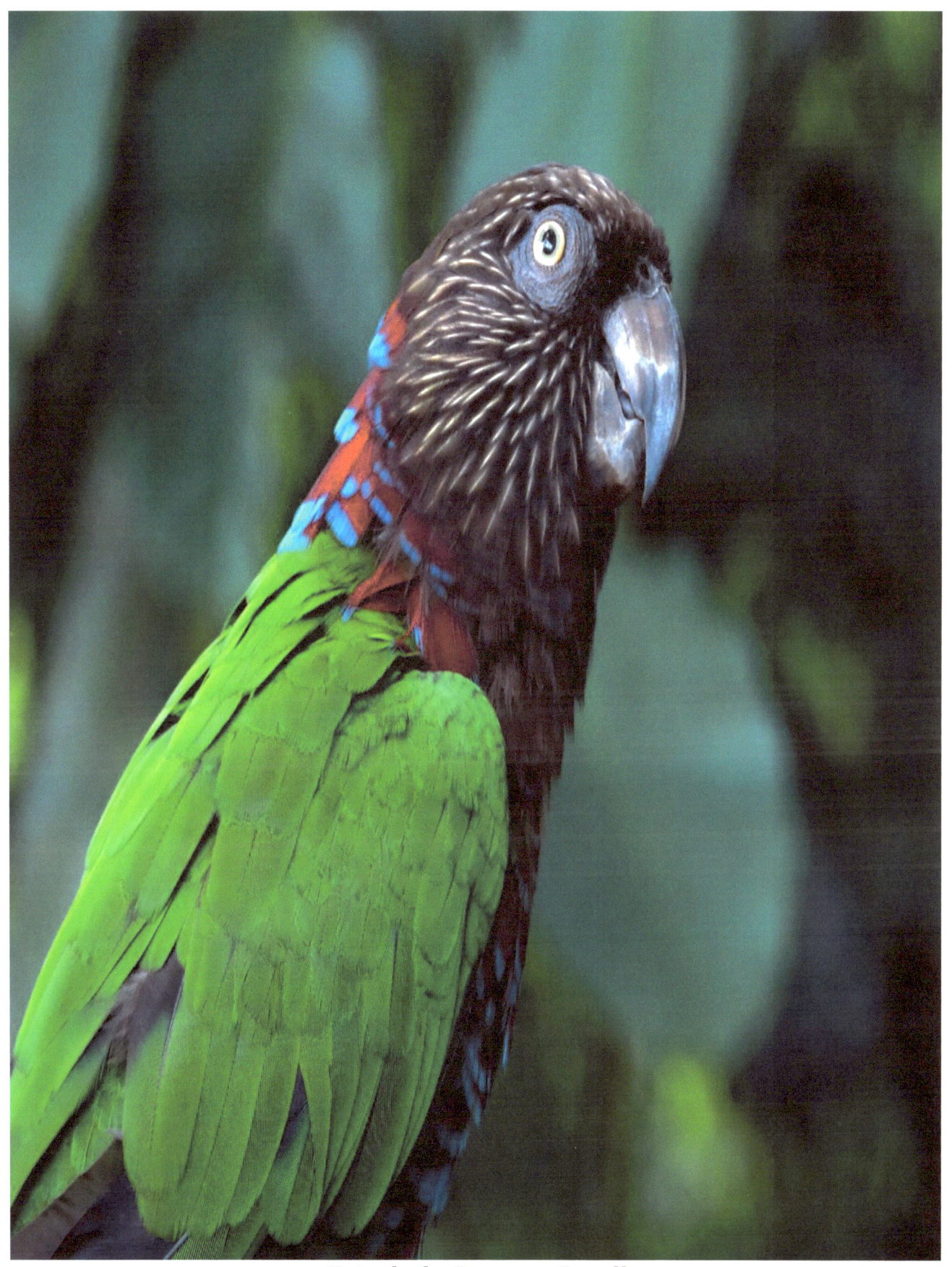

Estadode Parana, Brasil
Photographer: Dahiana Waszaj – Encarnacion, Paraguay

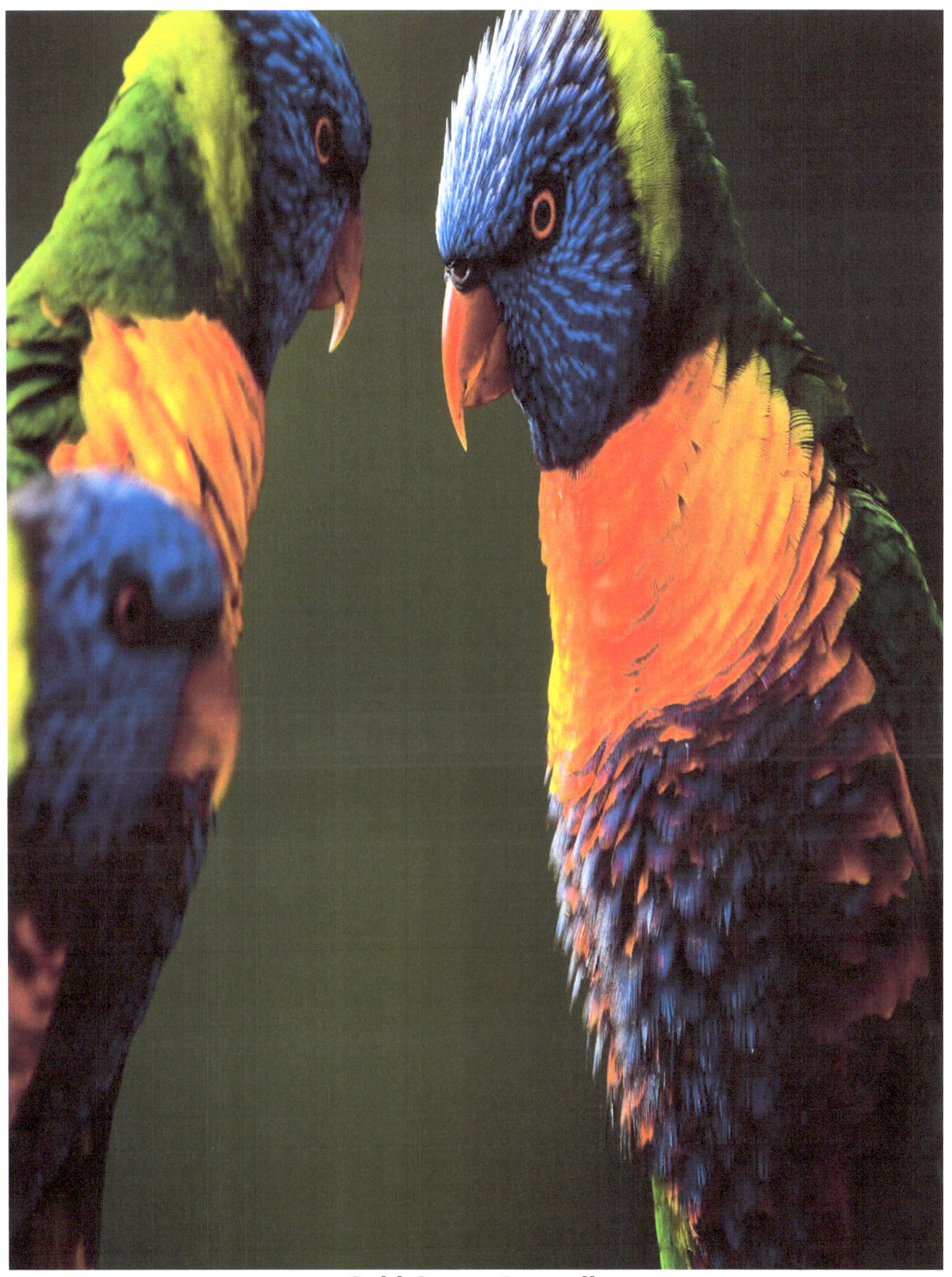

Gold Coast, Australia
Photographer: Damon Hall – Gold Coast, Australia

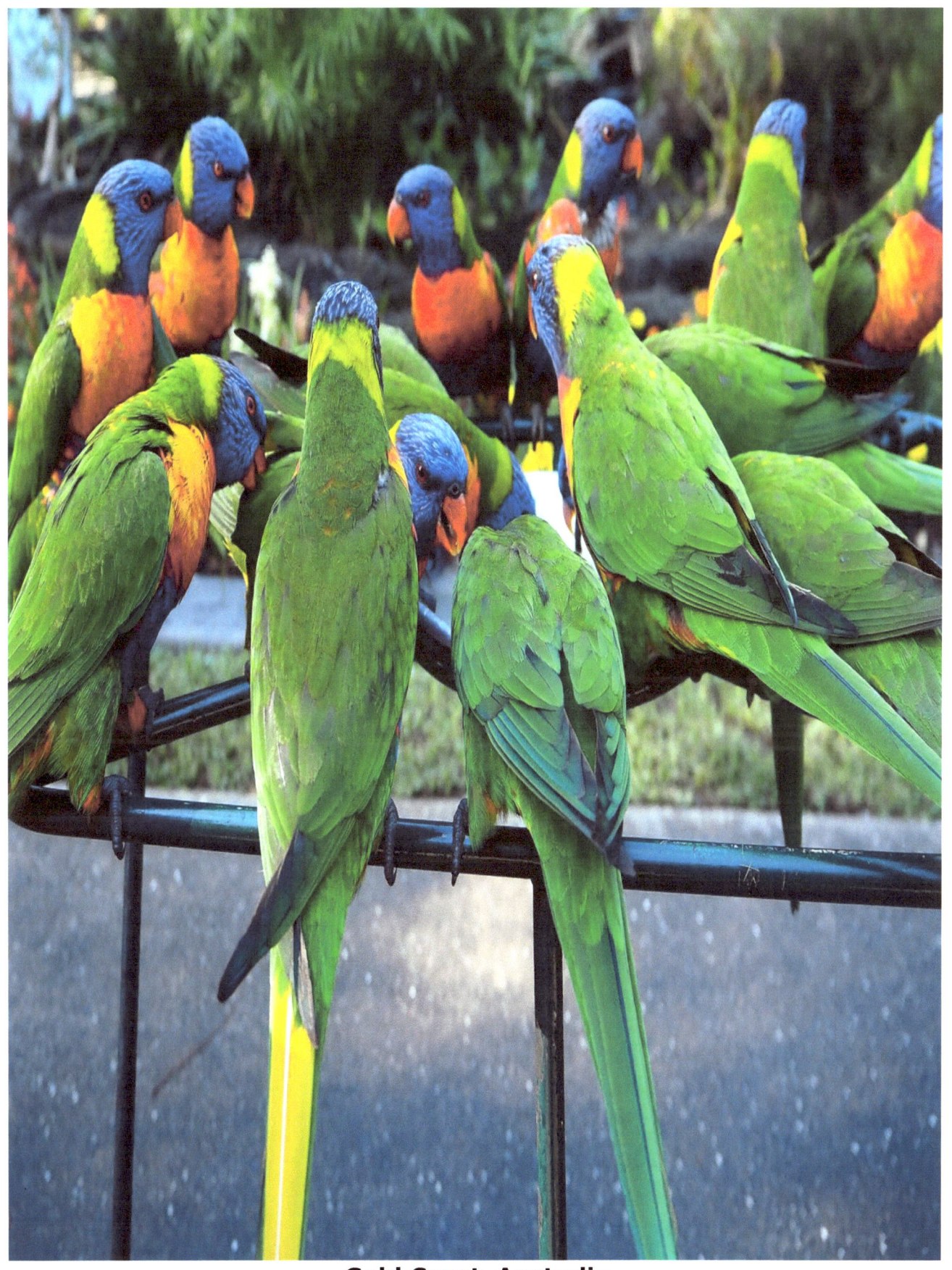

Gold Coast, Australia
Photographer: Deb Dowd, Queensland, Australia

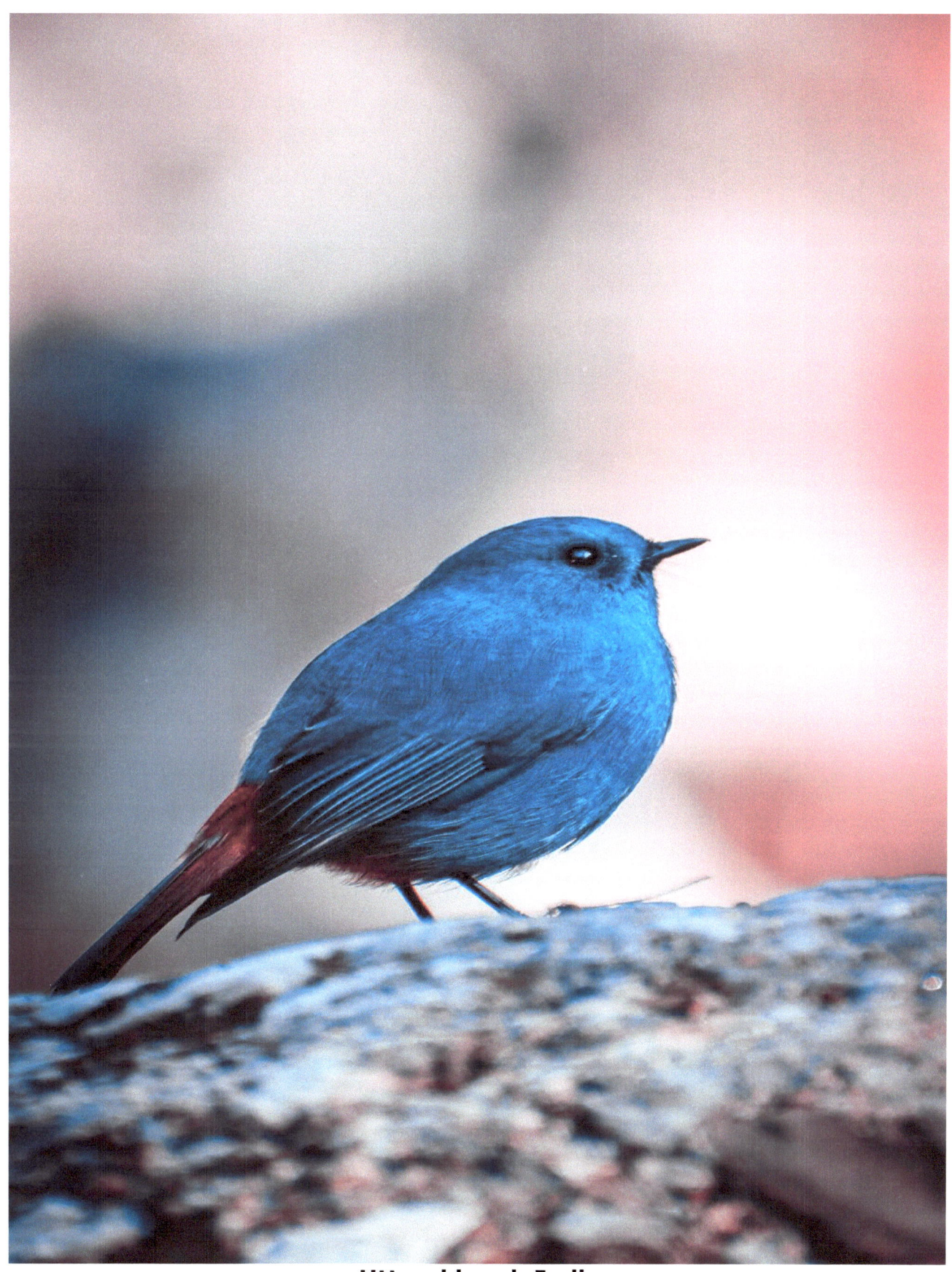

Uttarakhand, India
Photographer: Deepak Nautiyal - India

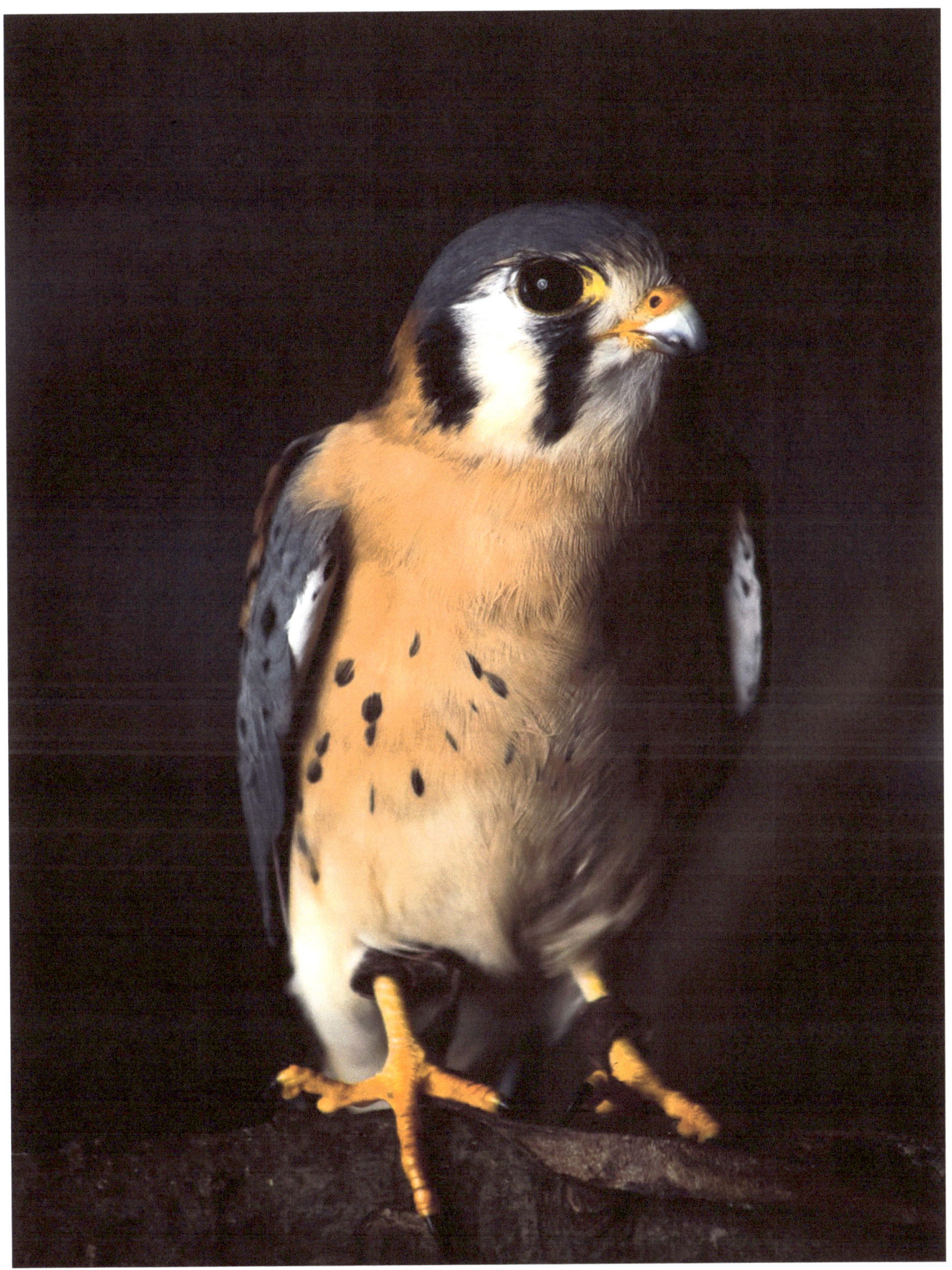

Photographer: Delaney Van – Austin, Texas

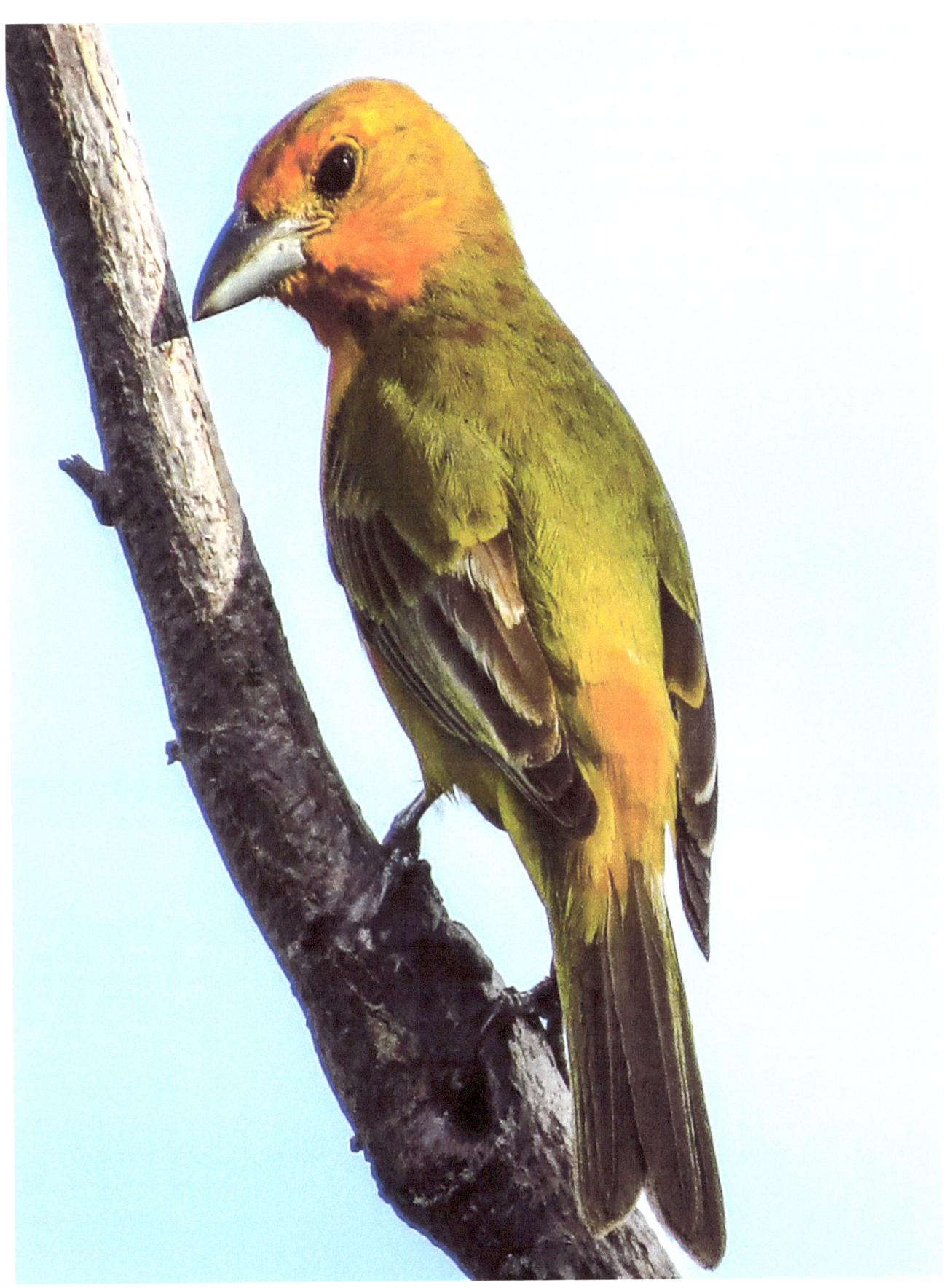

Photographer: Dieny Portinanni – Roraima, Brazil

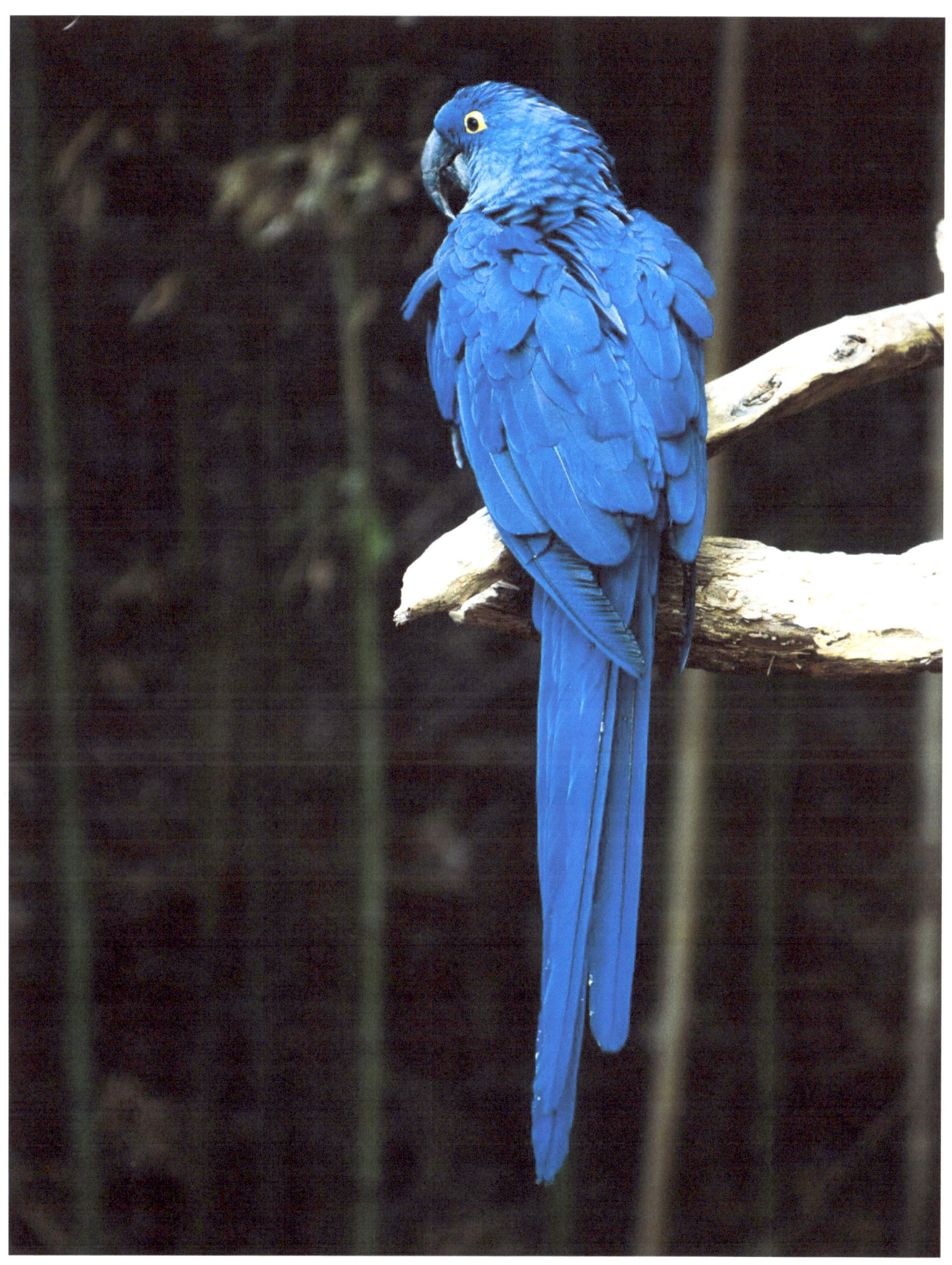

Photographer: Dominik Lange - Texas

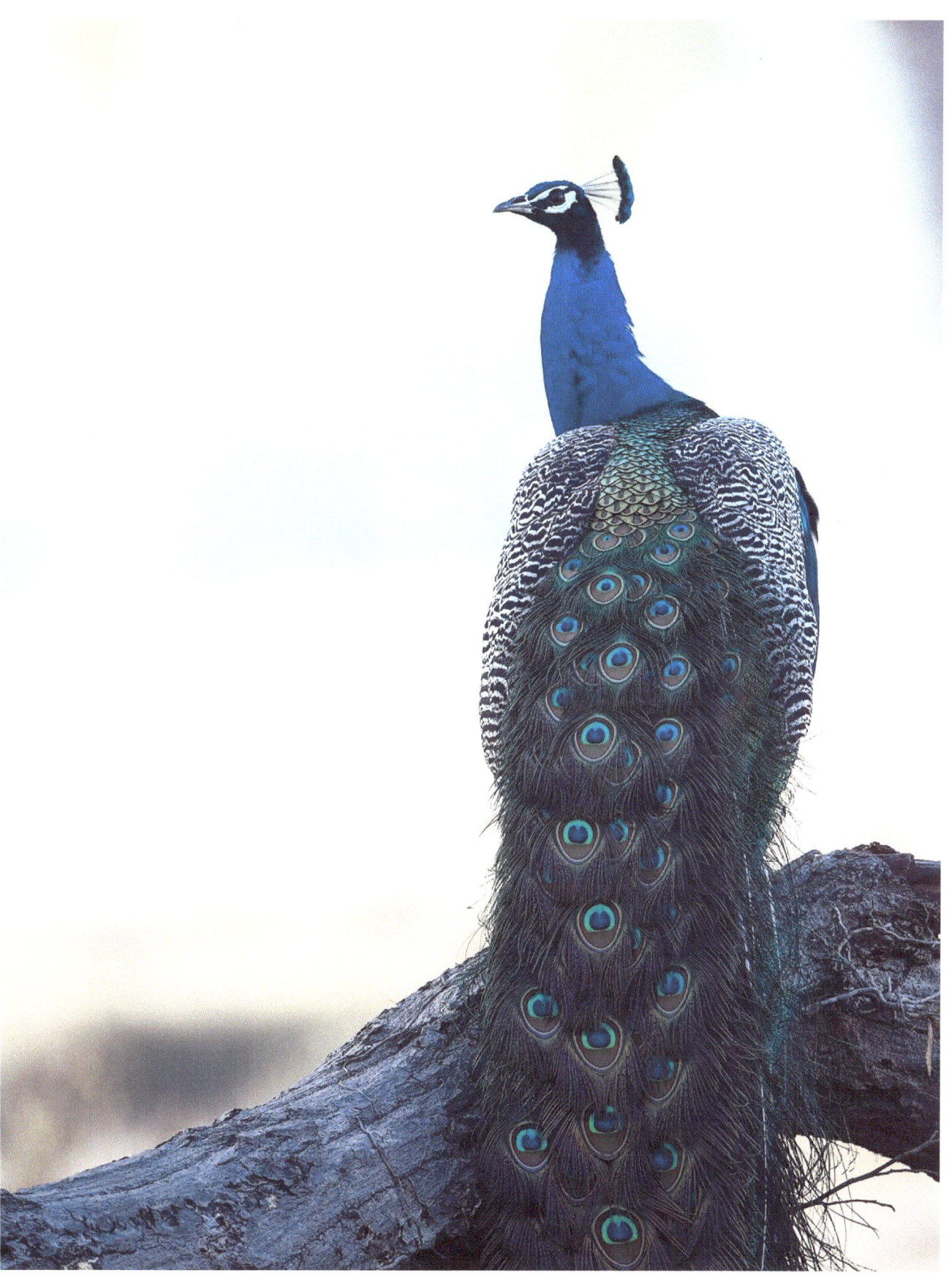

Photographer: Hans Veth

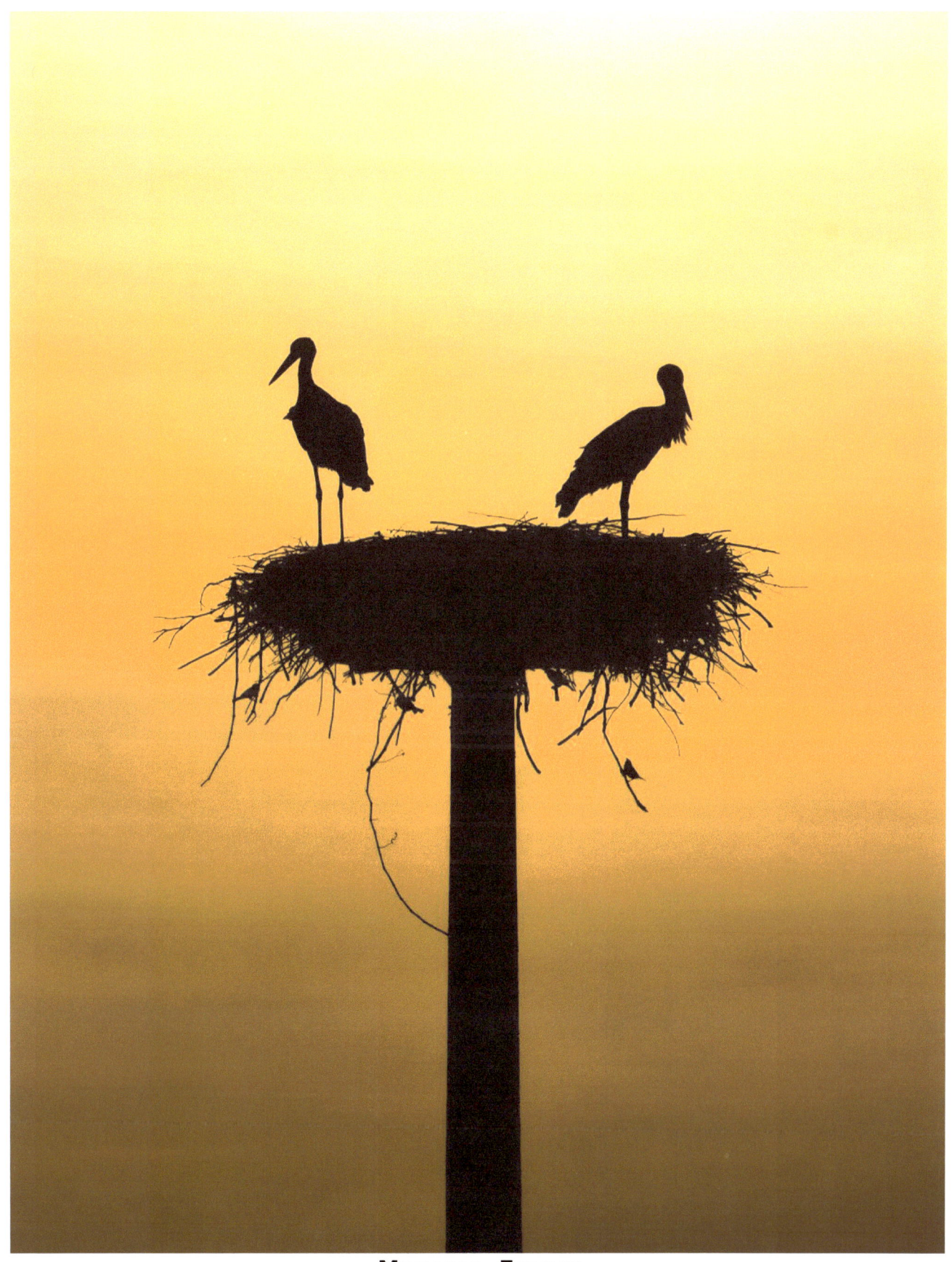

Mazeres, France
Photographer: Gregorie Bertrand

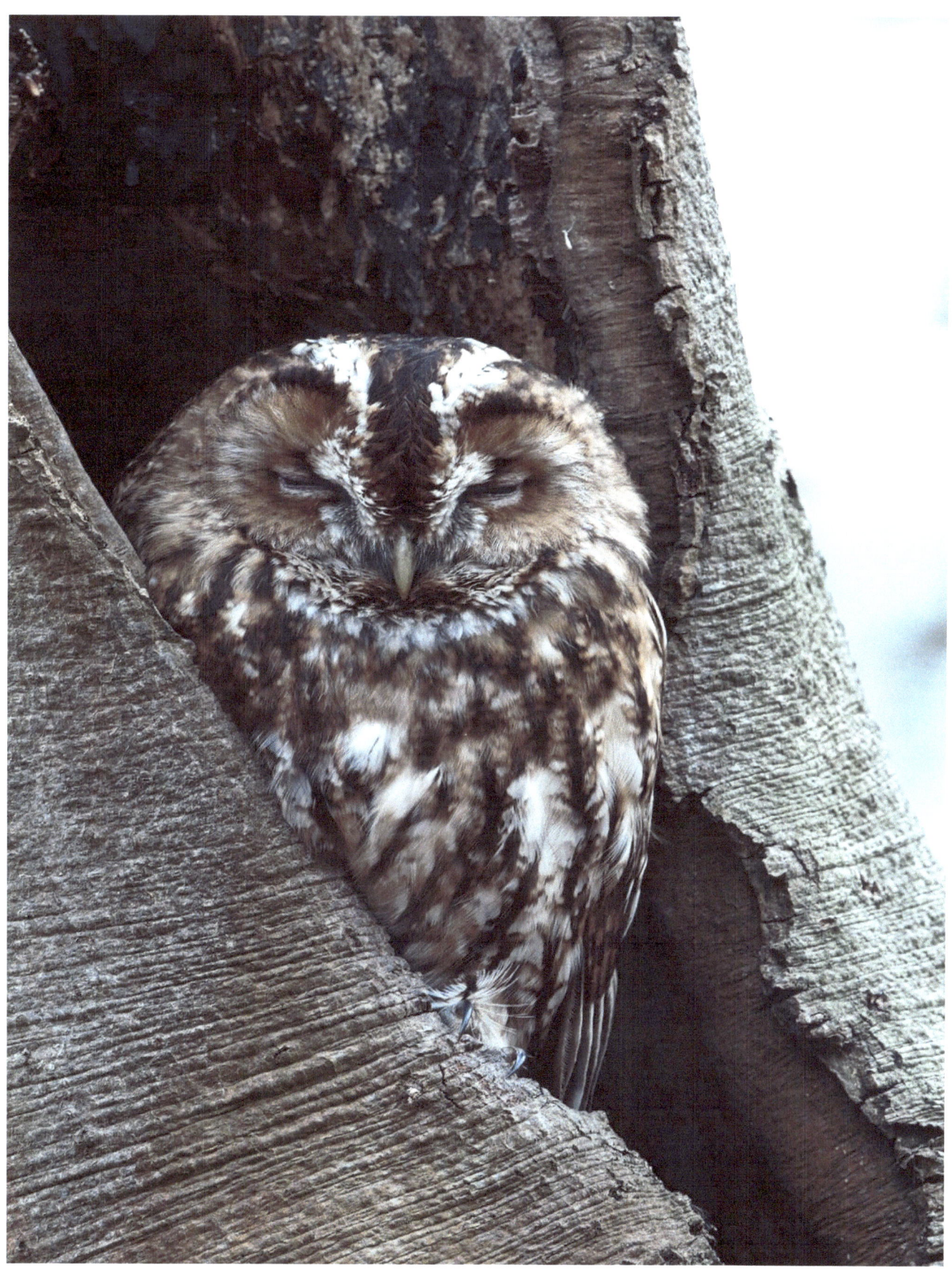

Photographer: Hans Veth

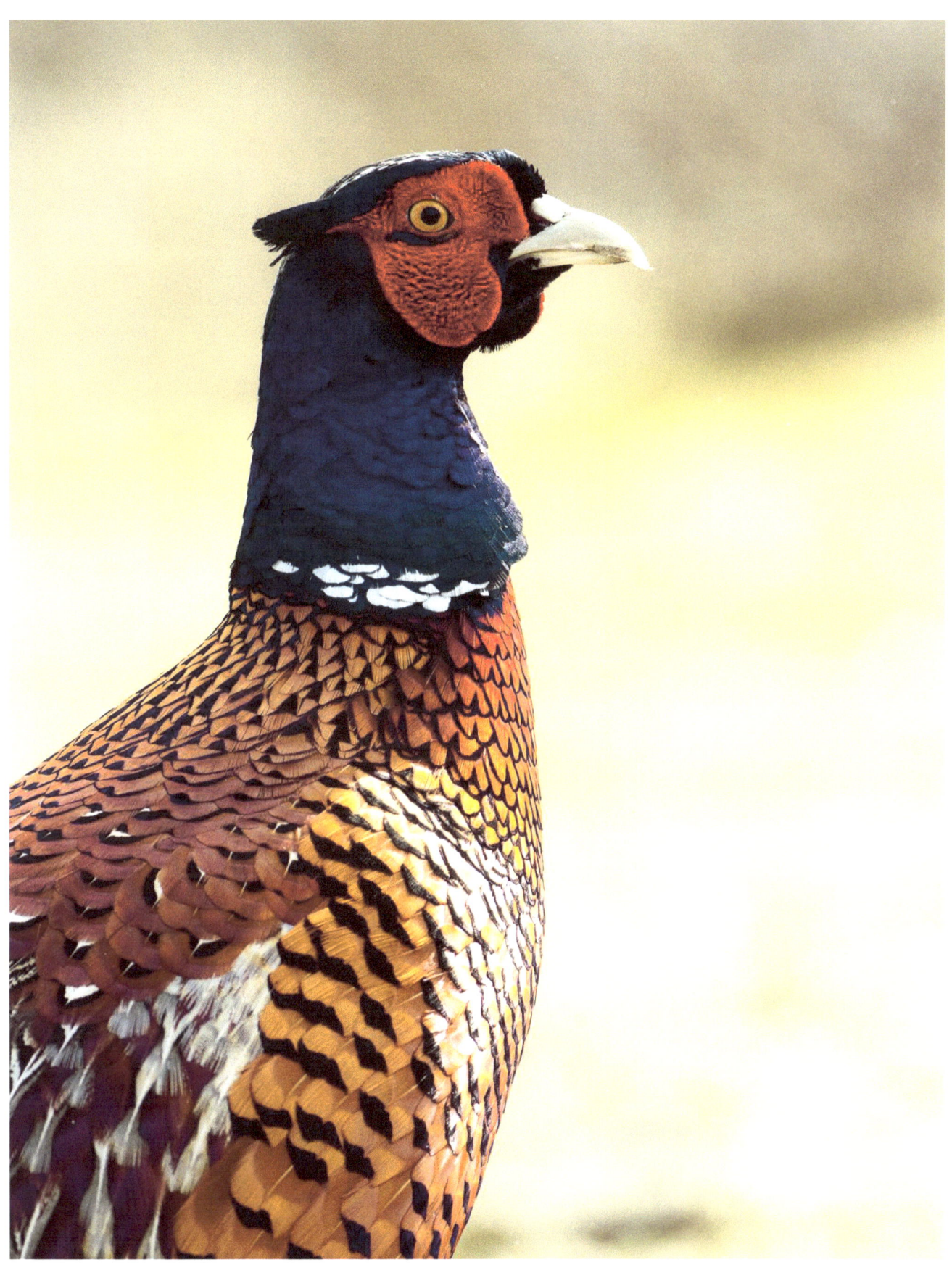

Photographer: Hans Veth

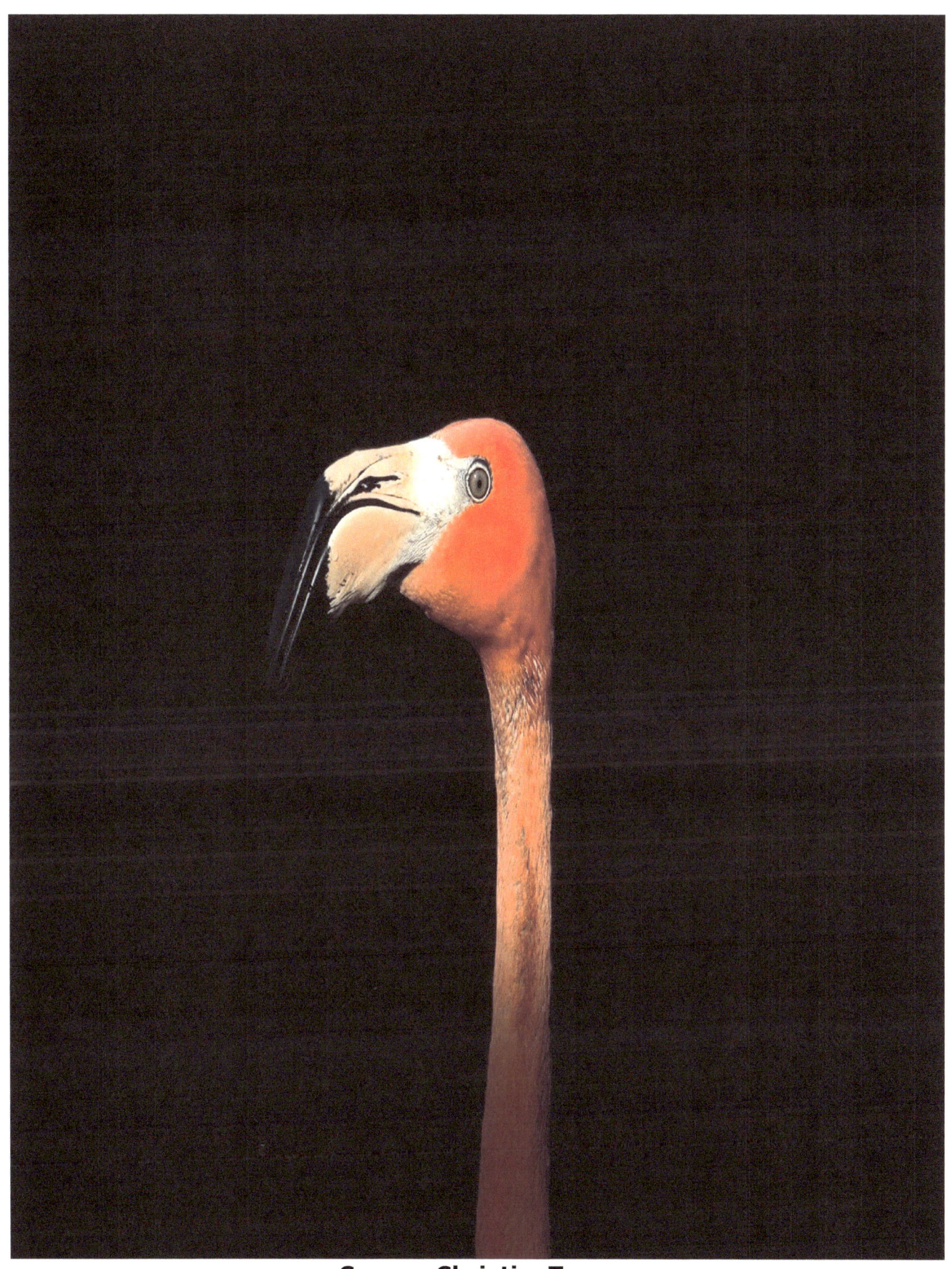

Corpus Christie, Texas
Photographer: James Lee – Southern California

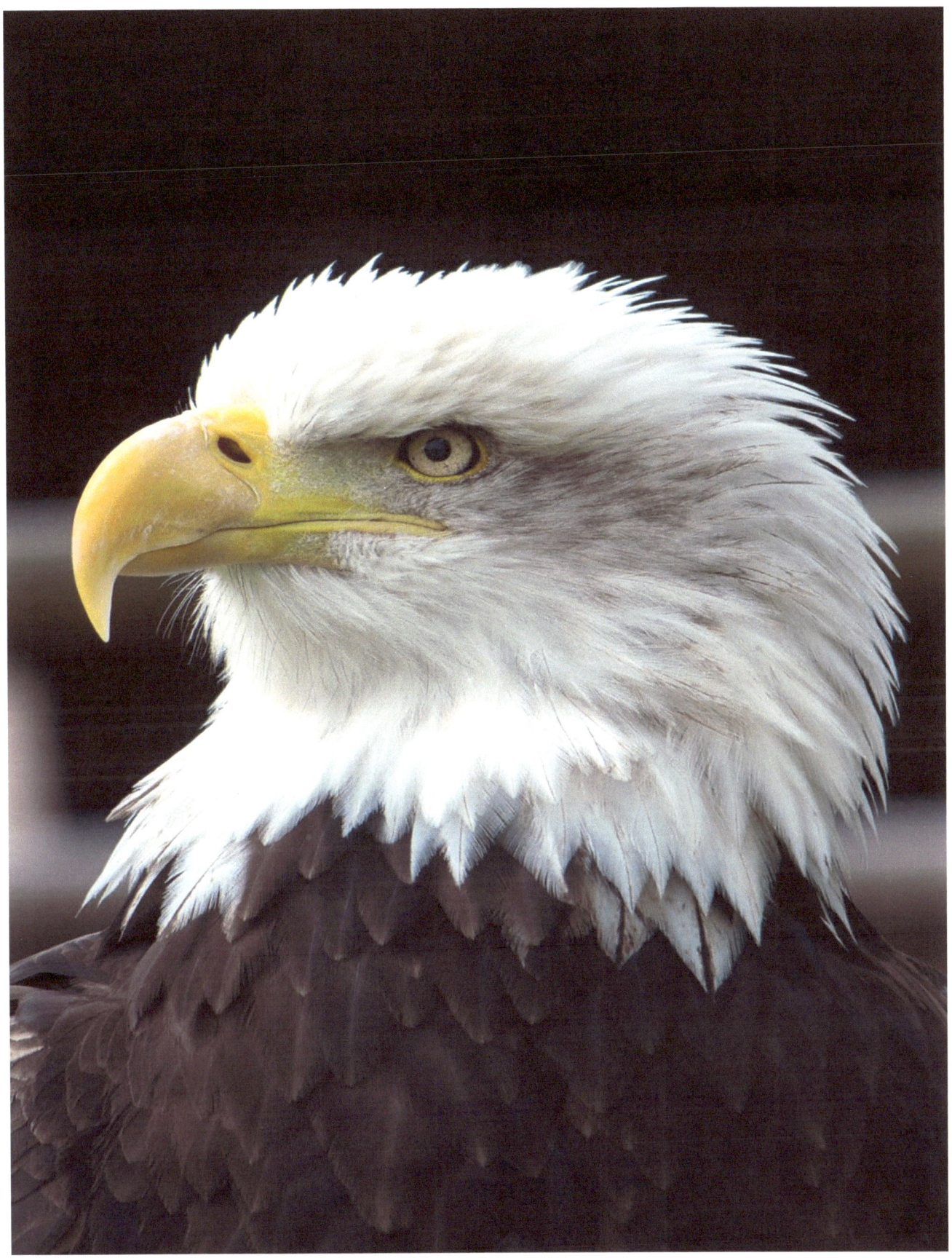

Warwick, UK
Photographer: James Newcombe – High Peak, UK

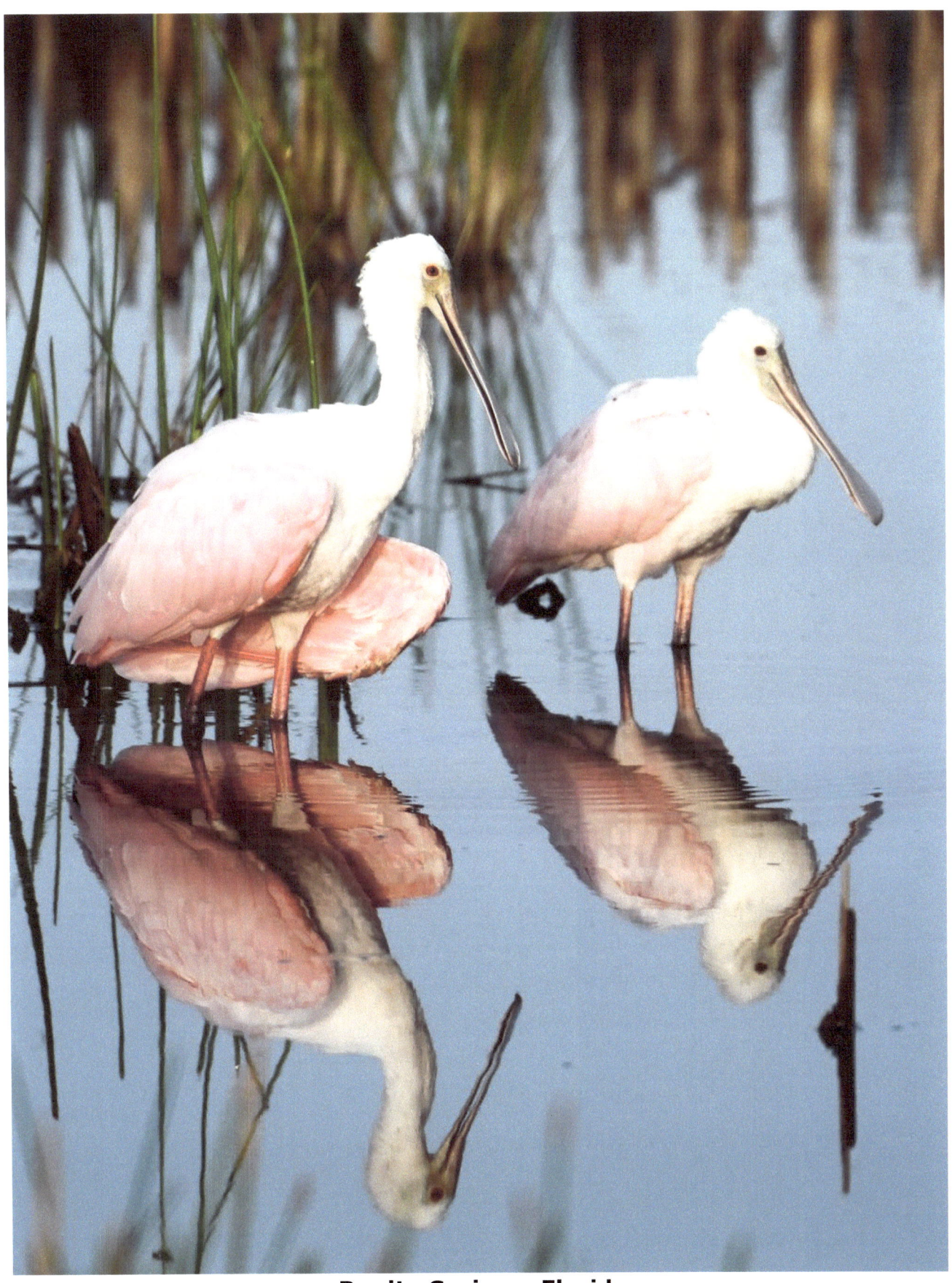

Bonita Springs, Florida
Photographer: J Dean

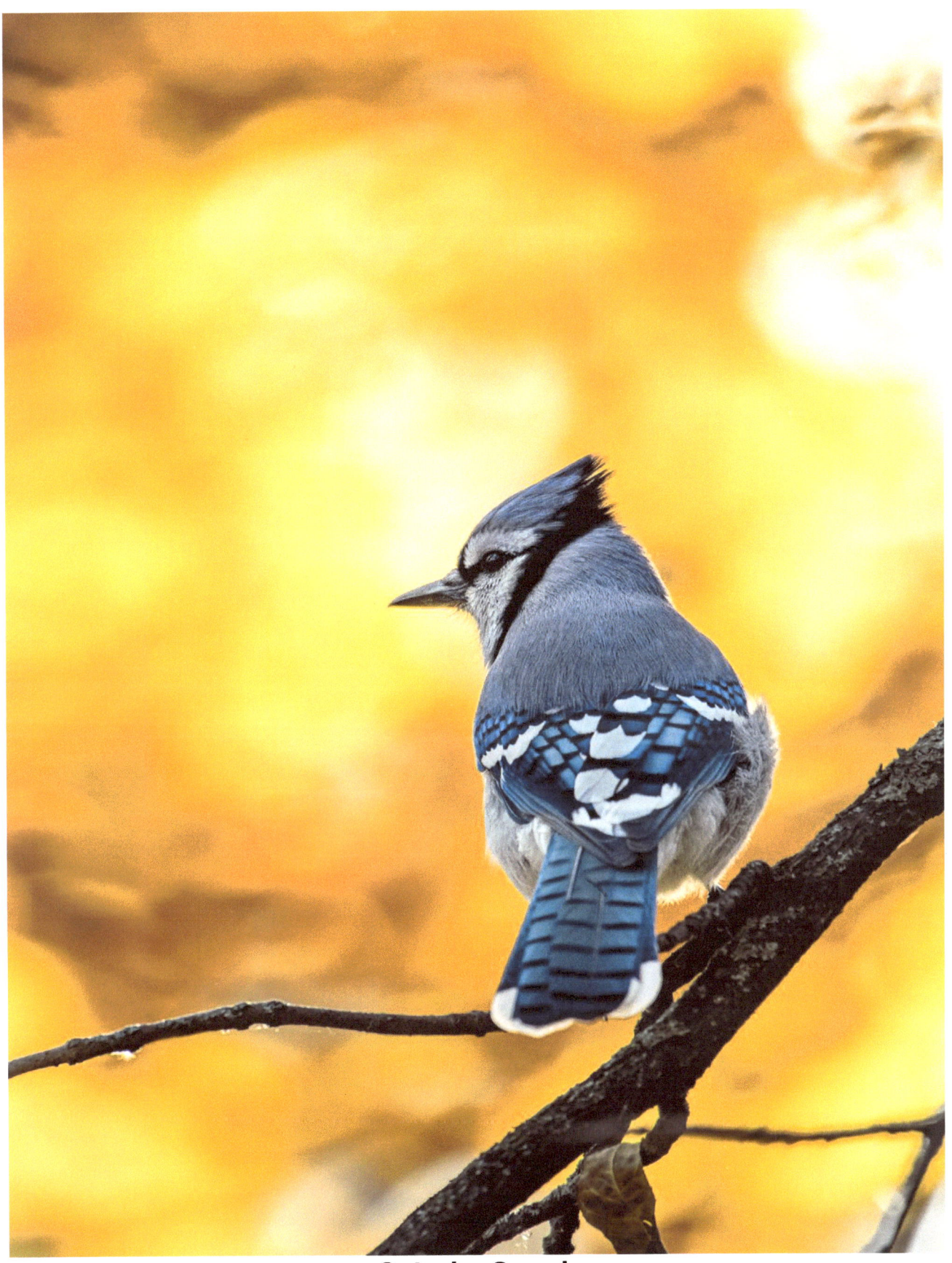

Ontario, Canada
Photographer: Jeremy Hynes – Ontario, Canada

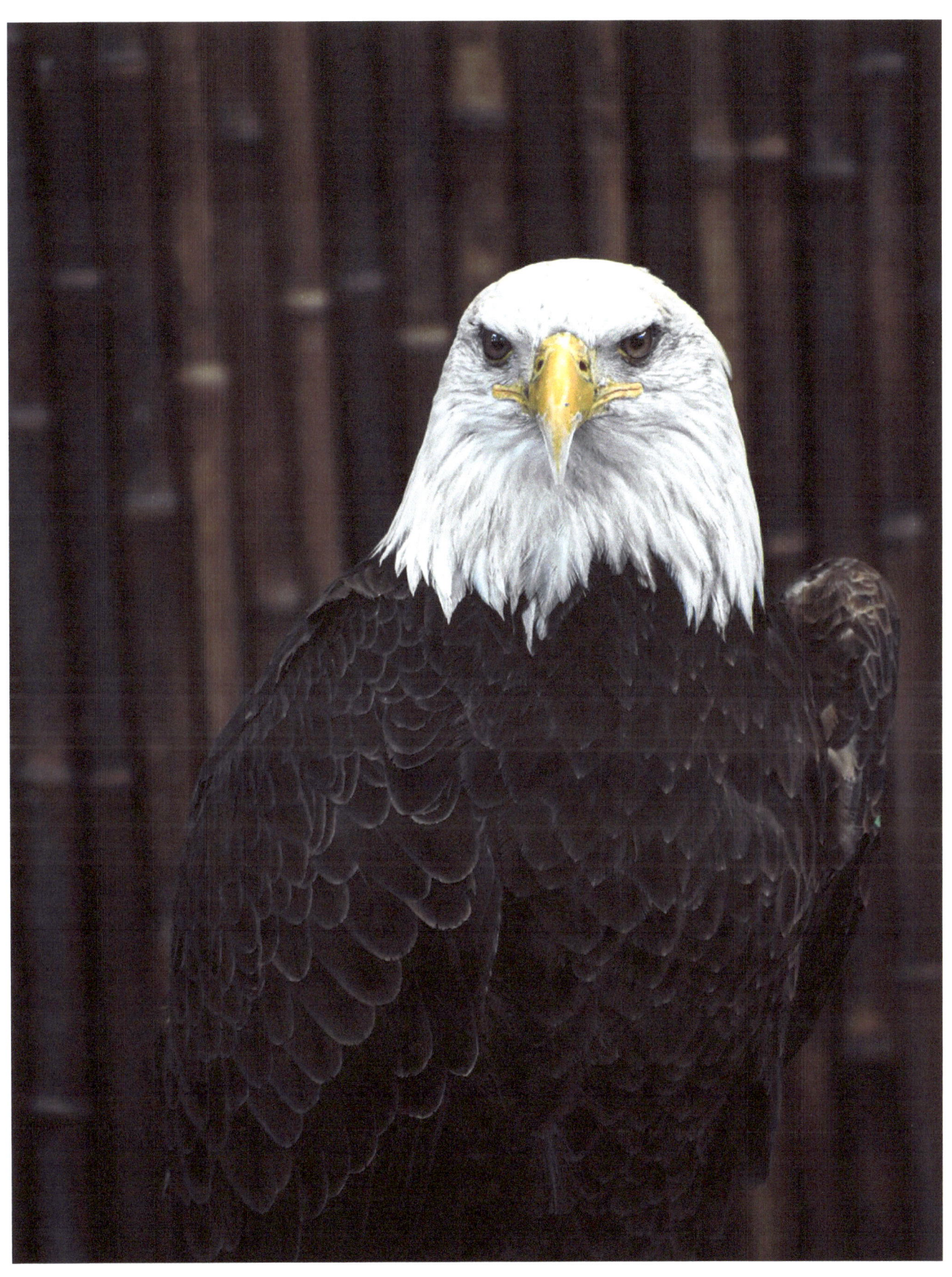

Photographer: Johnathan Ciarocca – Wilmington, North Carolina

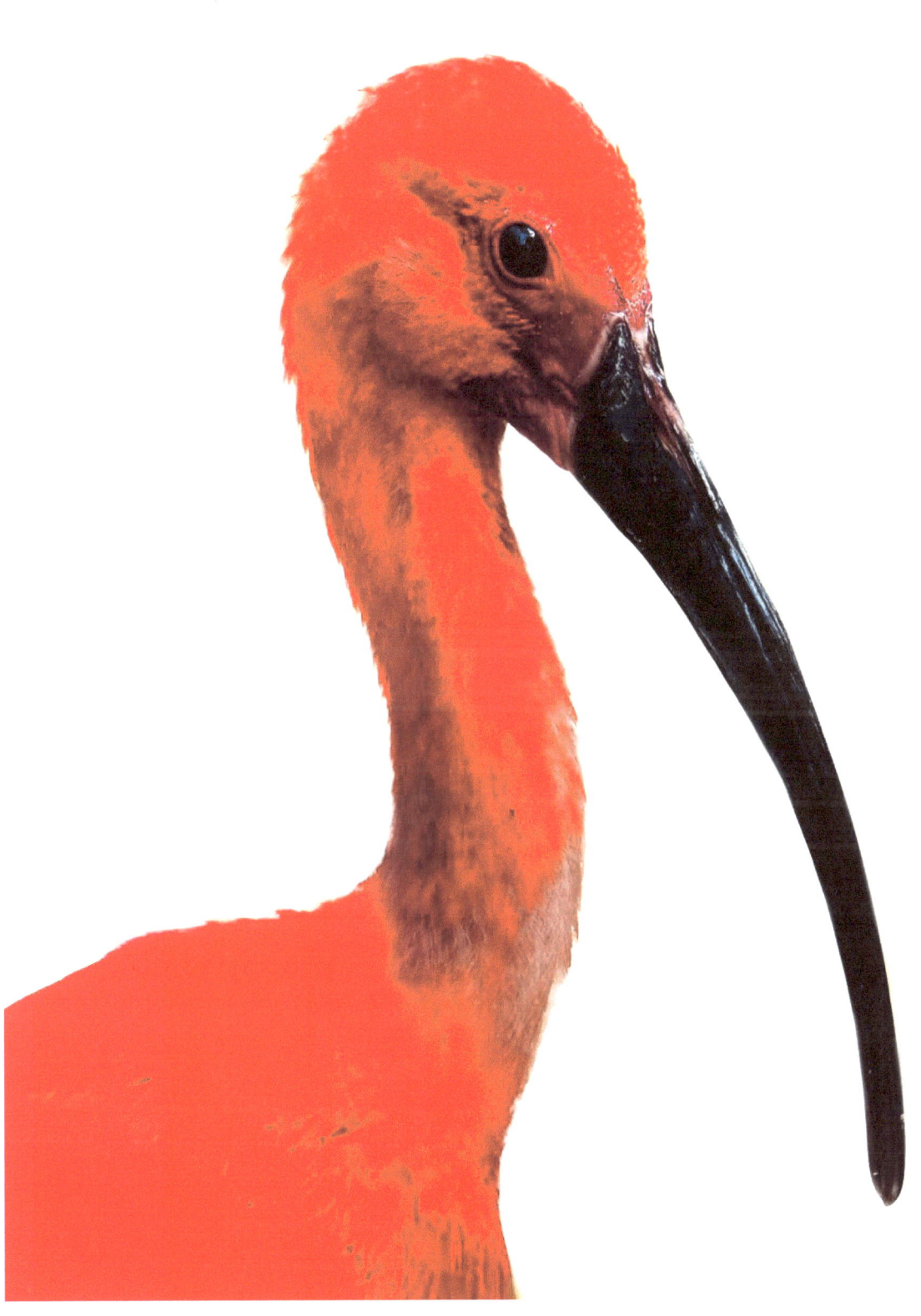

Photographer: John McMahon

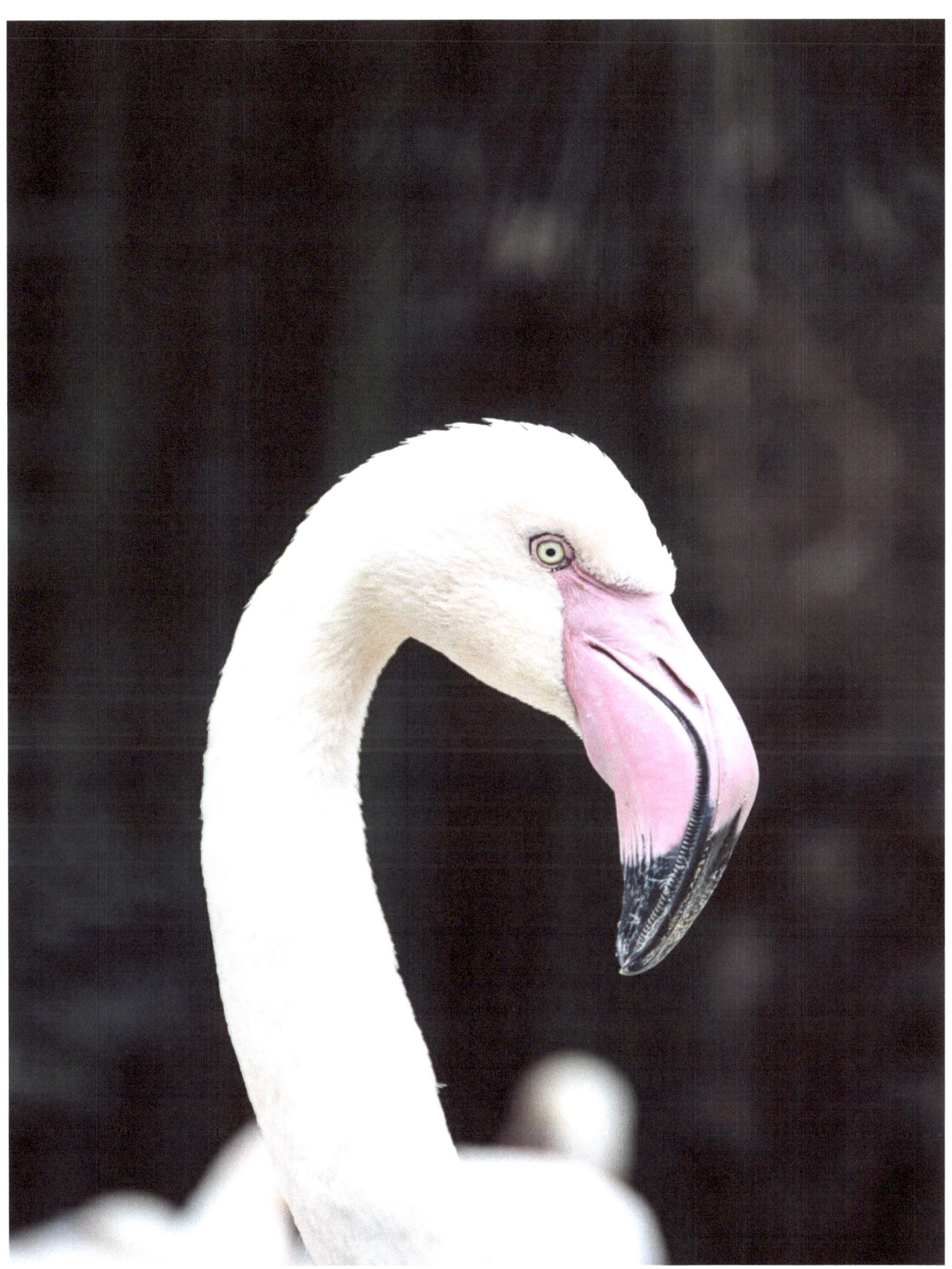

Photographer: Luca Ambrosi – Verona, Italy

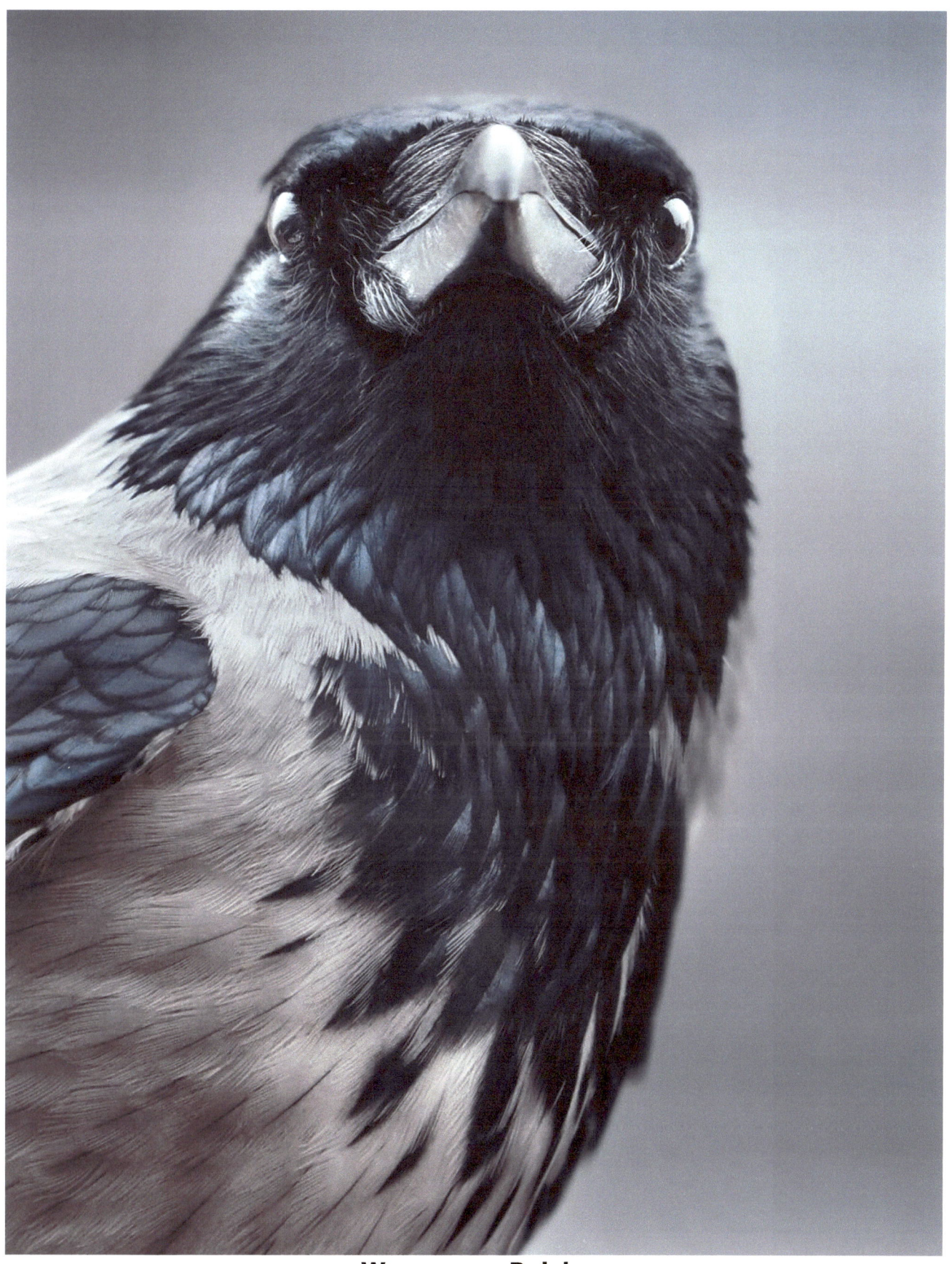

Warszawa, Polska
Photographer: Lukasz Rawa

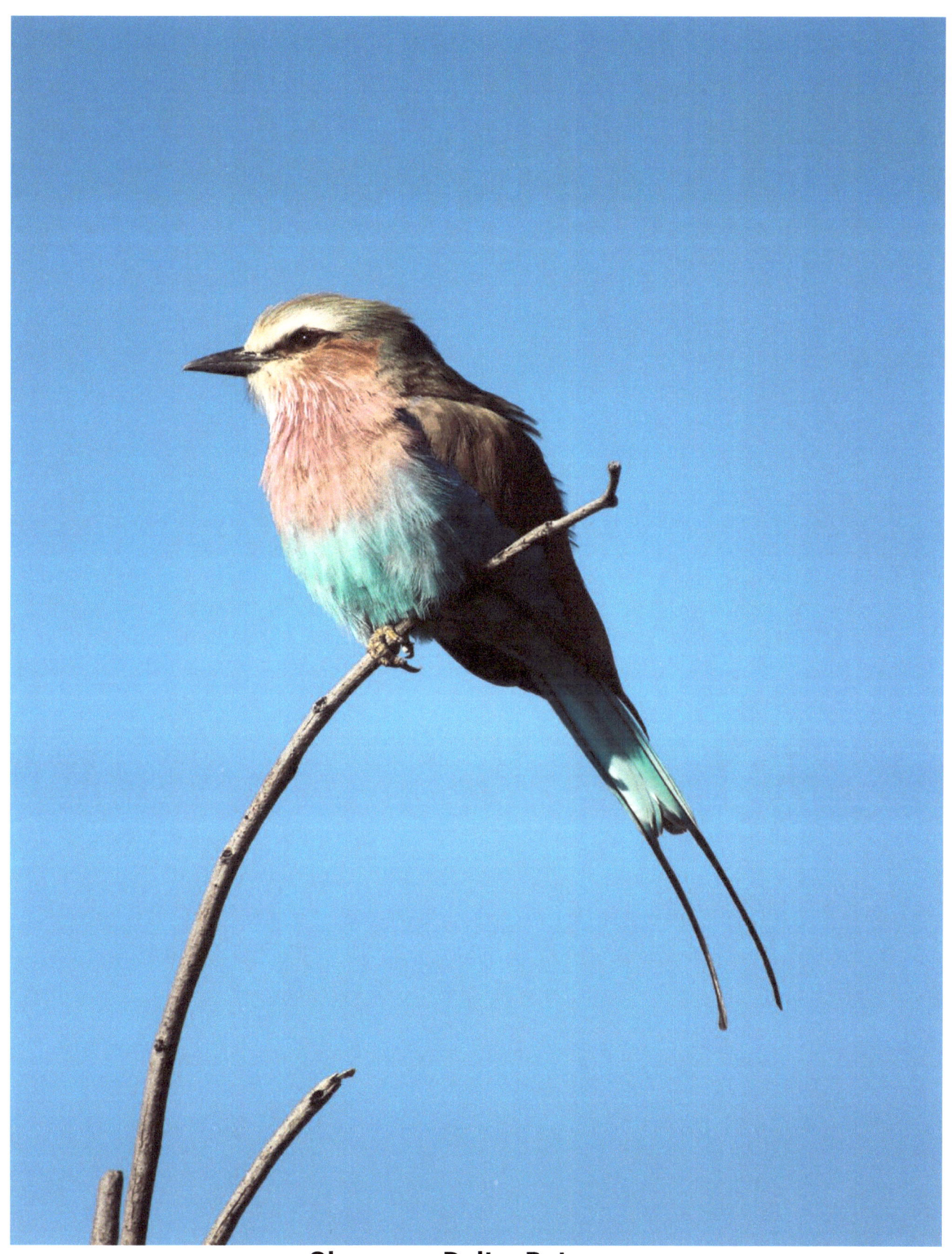

Okavango Delta, Botswana
Photographer: Madiba de African Inspiration, Leipzig, Germany

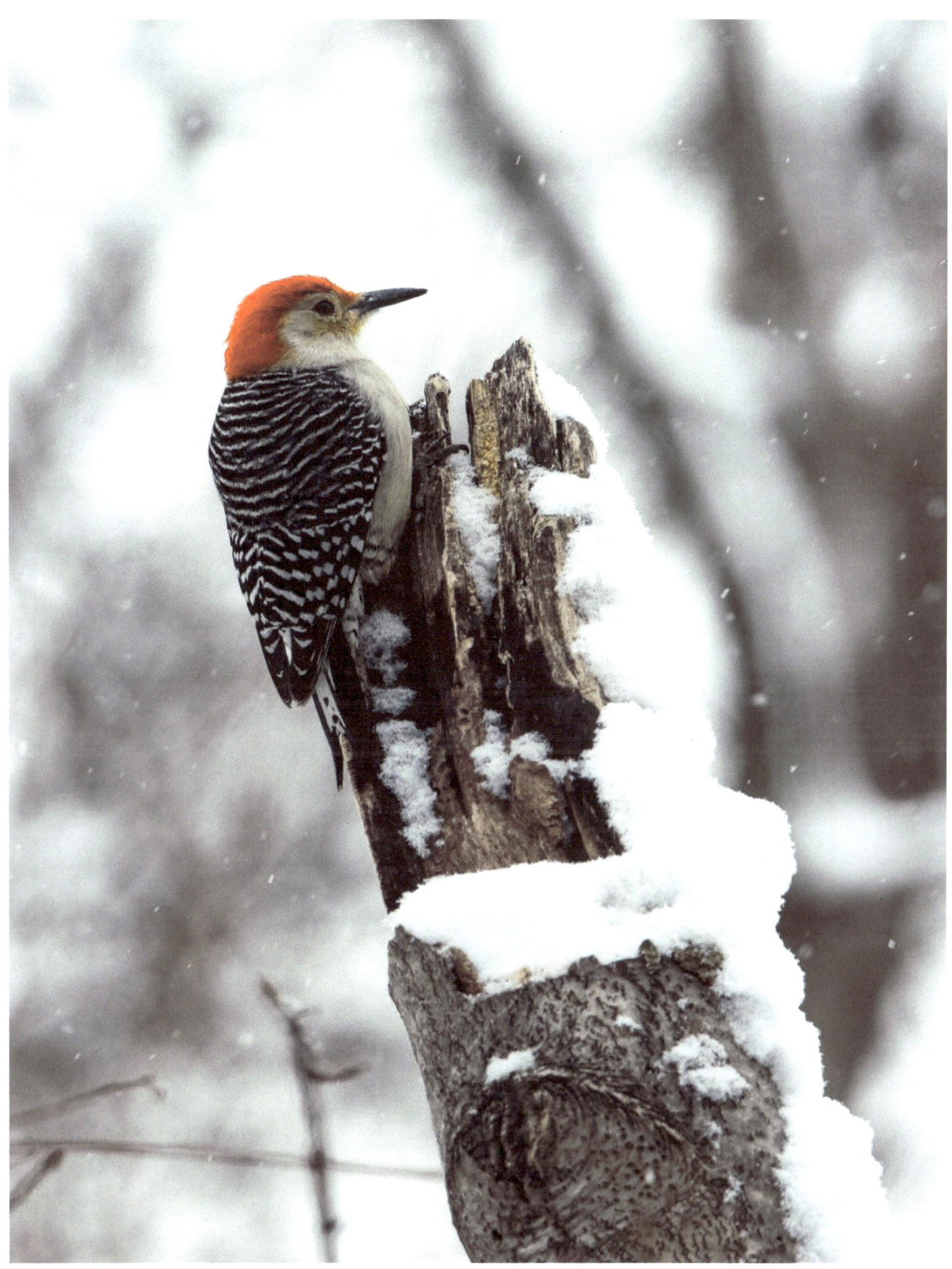

Photographer: Mark Olsen – Boston, Massachusetts

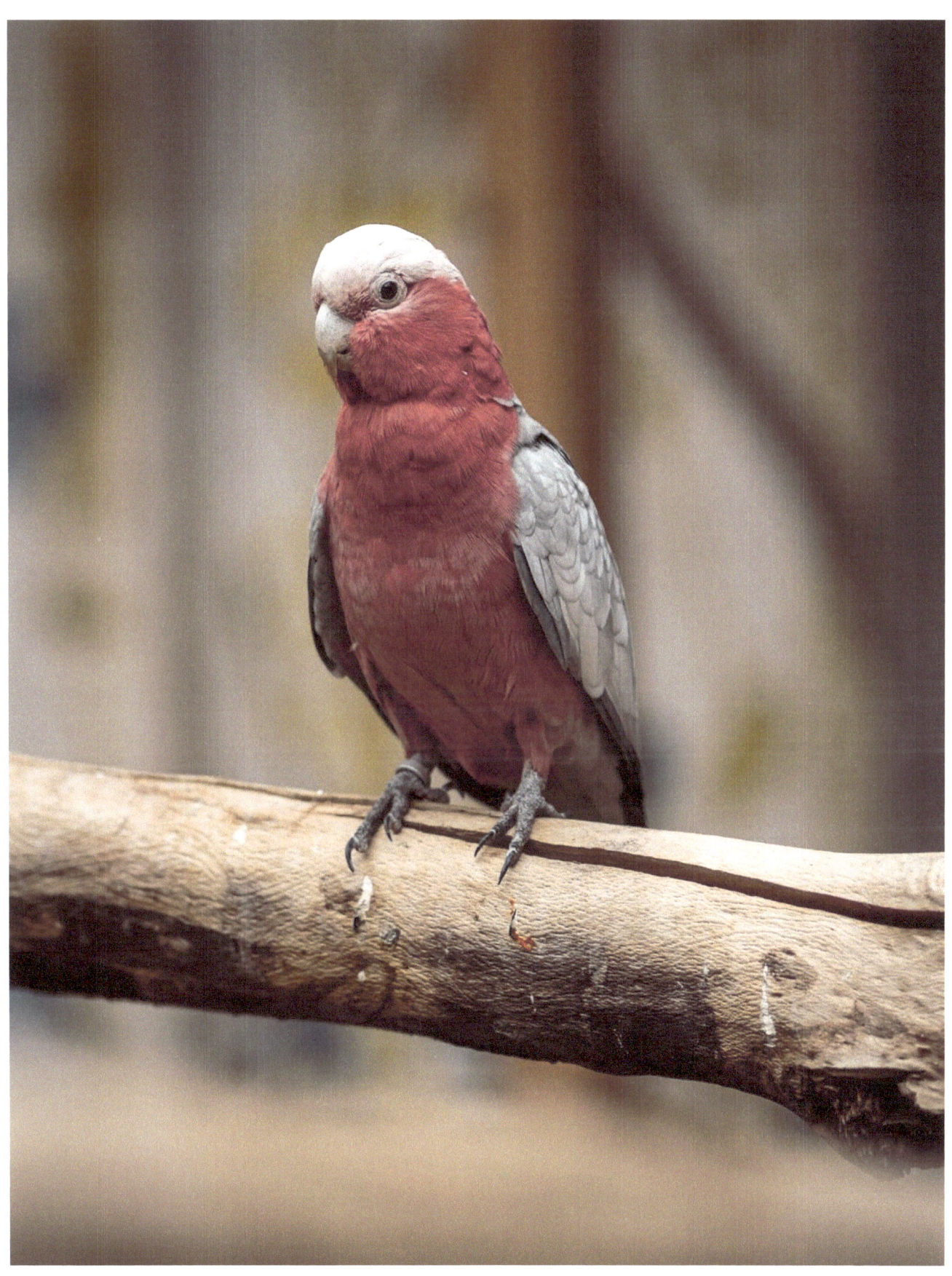

Photographer: Mateusz

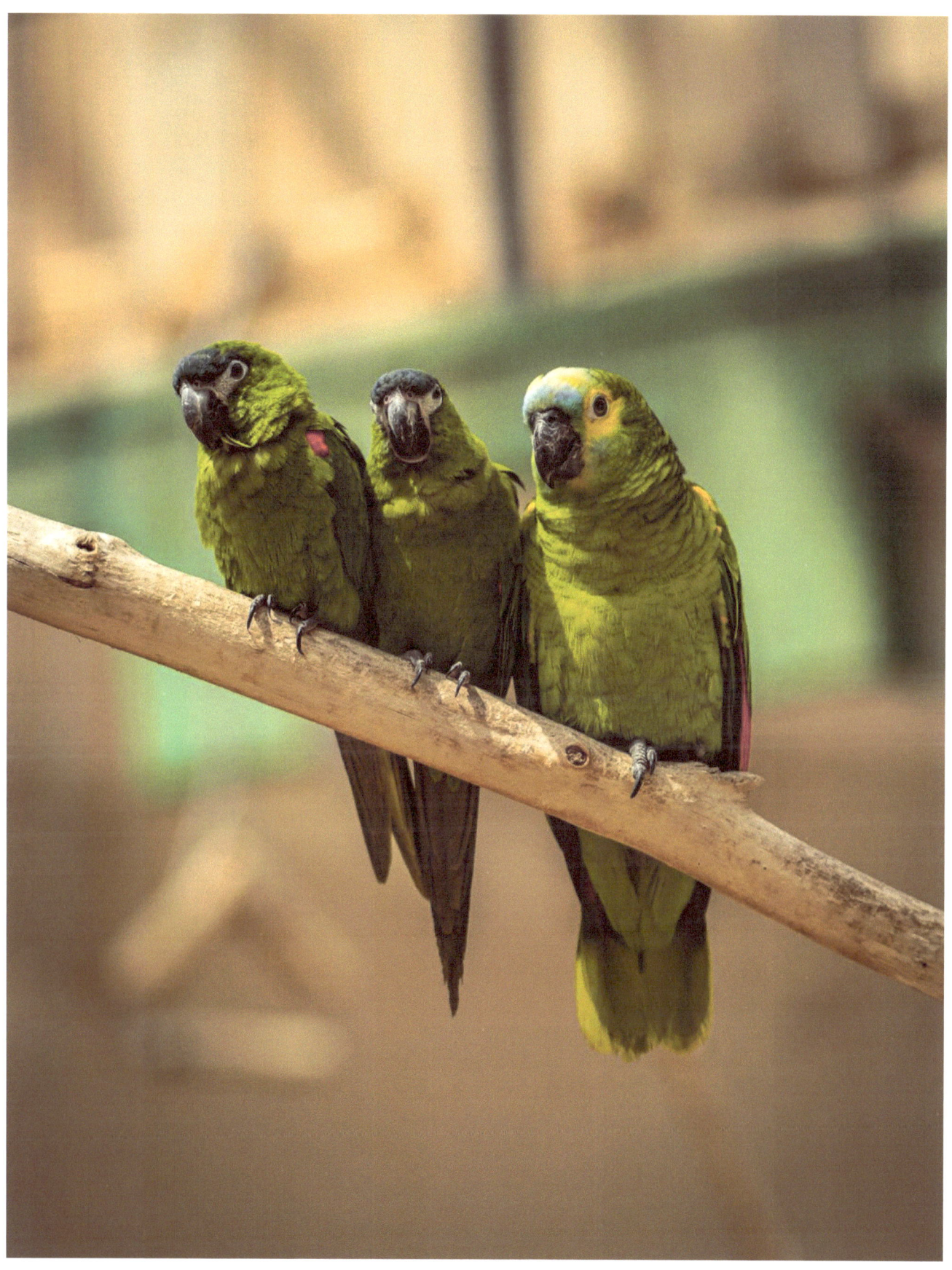

Photographer: Mateusz

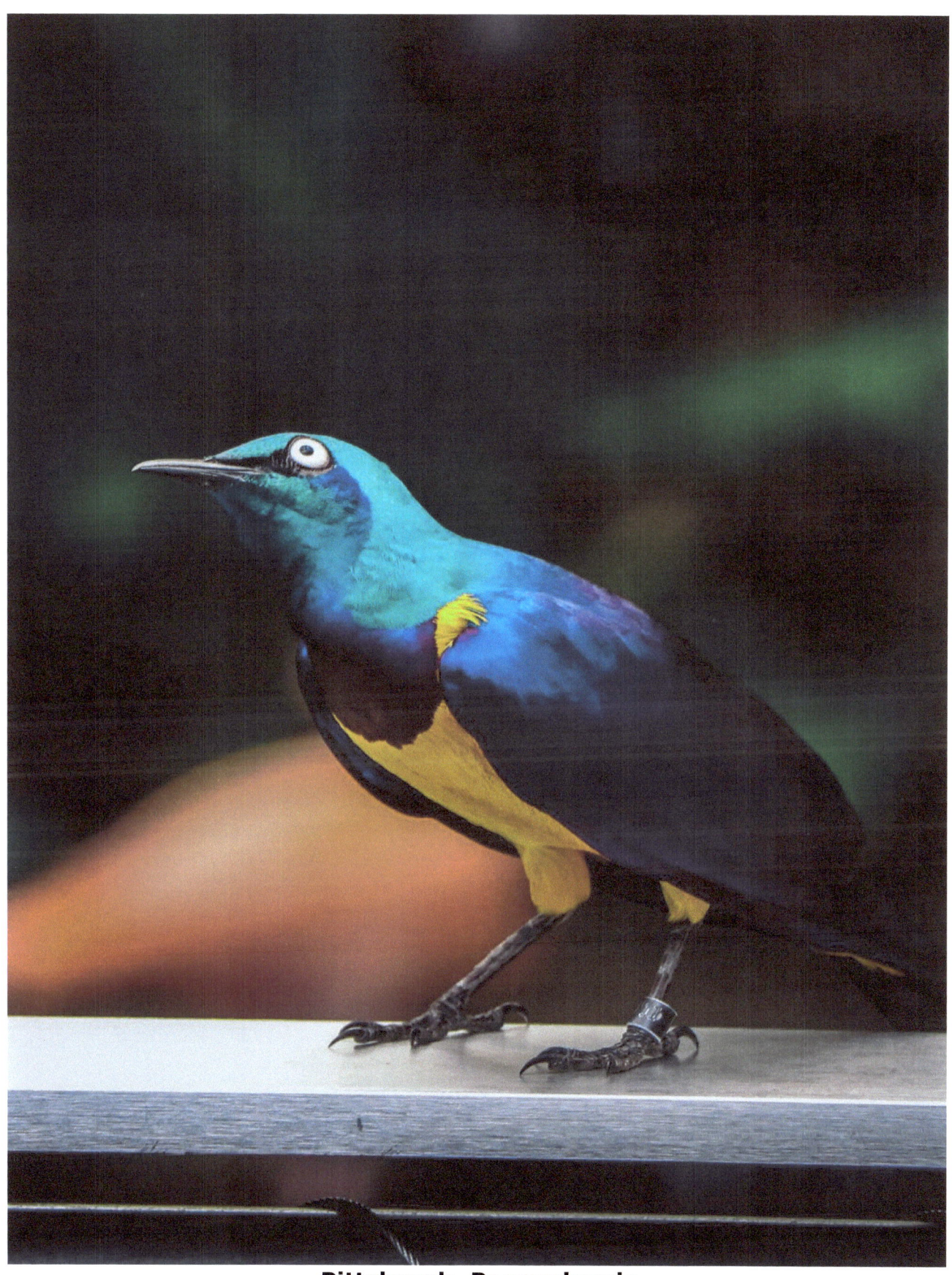

Pittsburgh, Pennsylvania
Photographer: Mingjun Liu

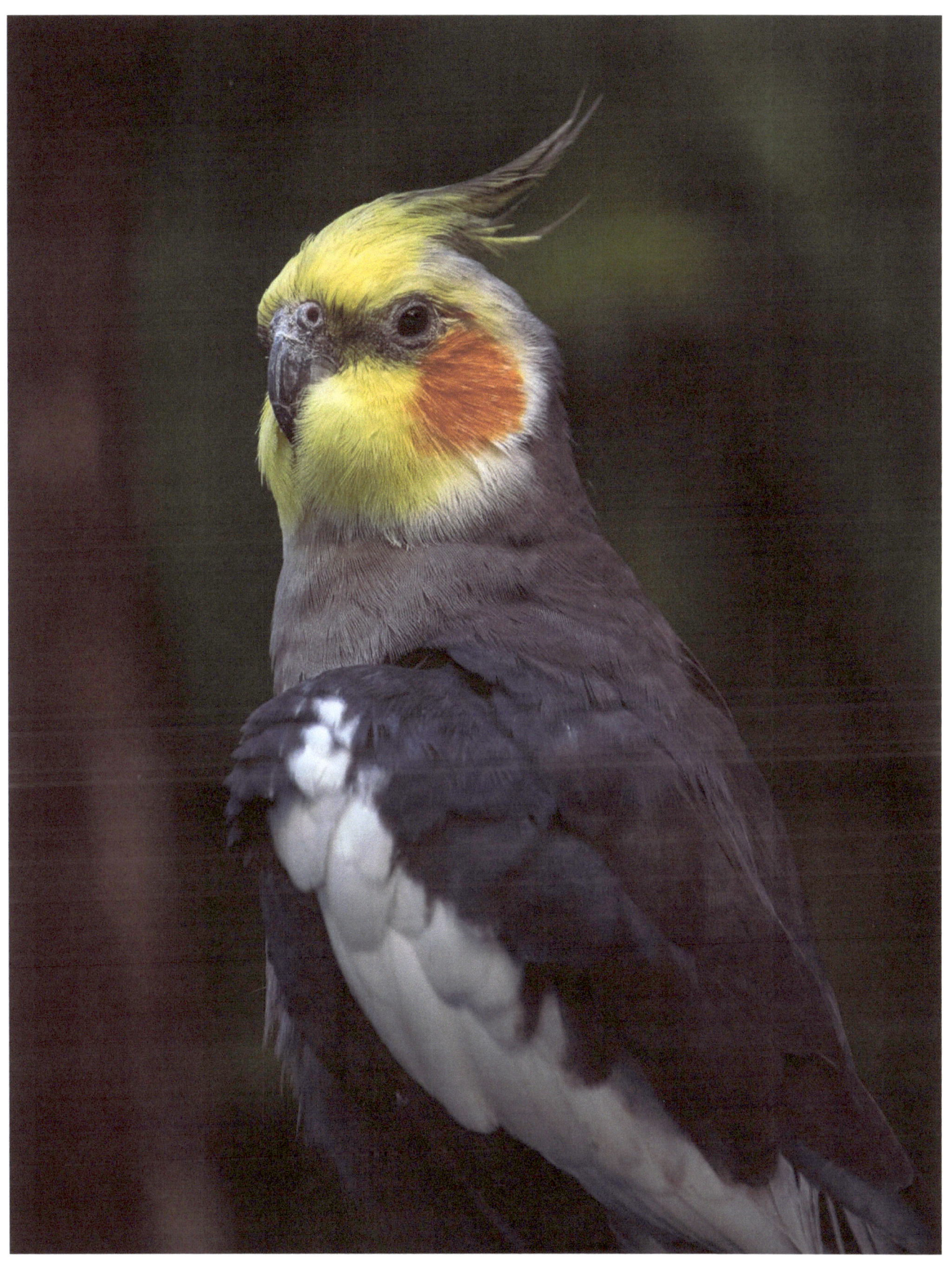

Photographer: Mohamed Elsayed – Alberta, Canada

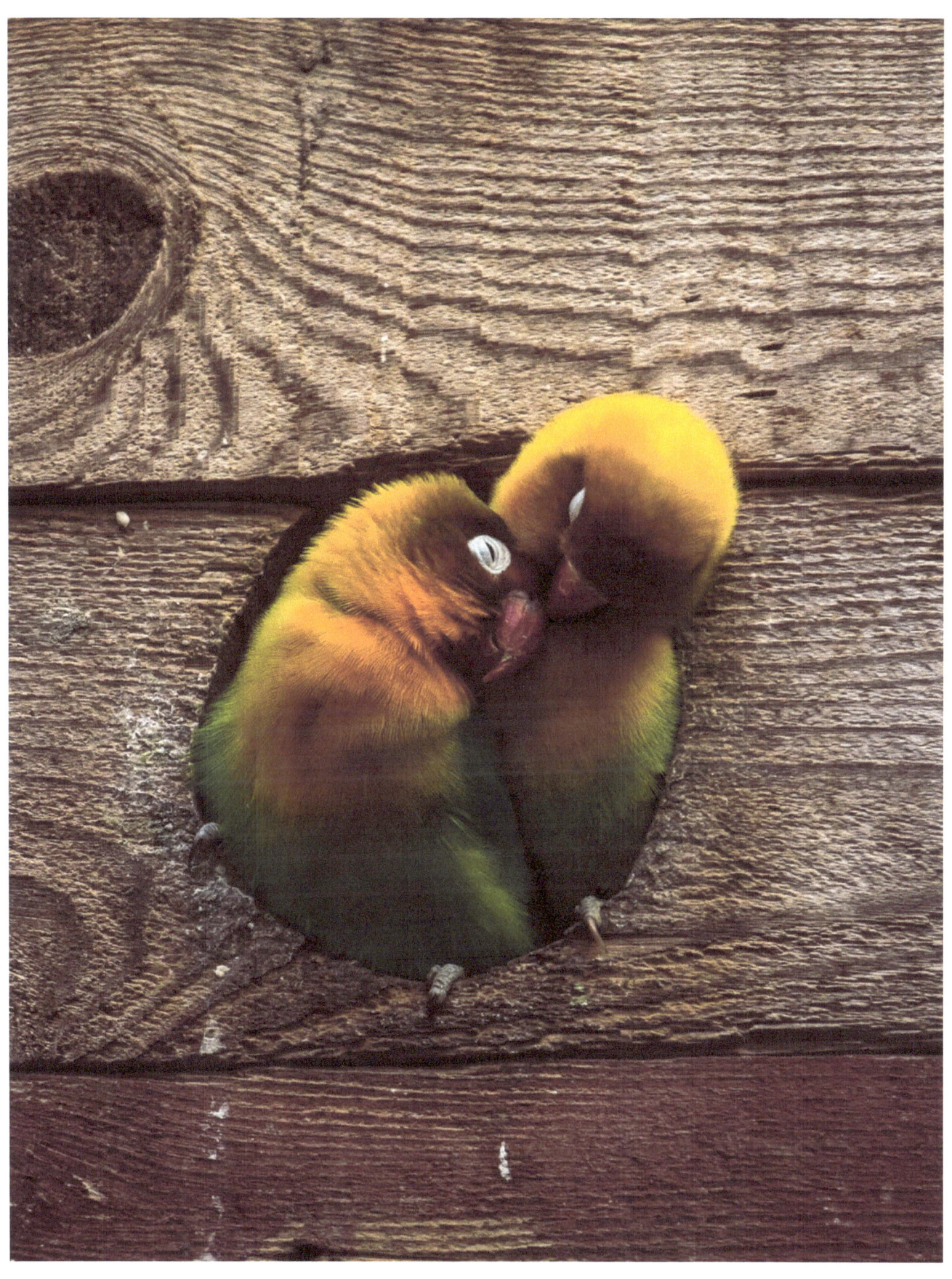

Photographer: Mohamed Elsayed – Alberta, Canada

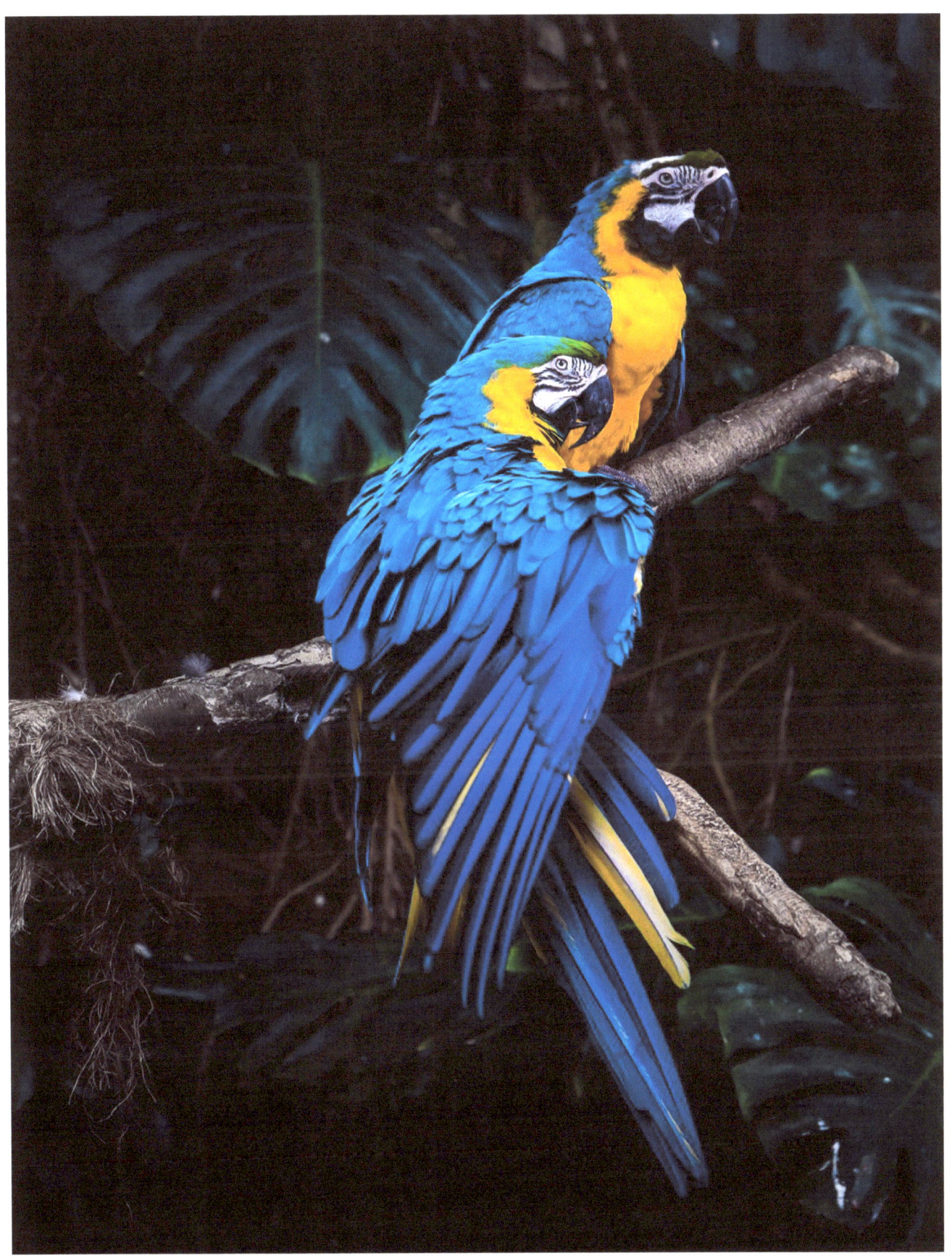

Photographer: Naser Tamimi

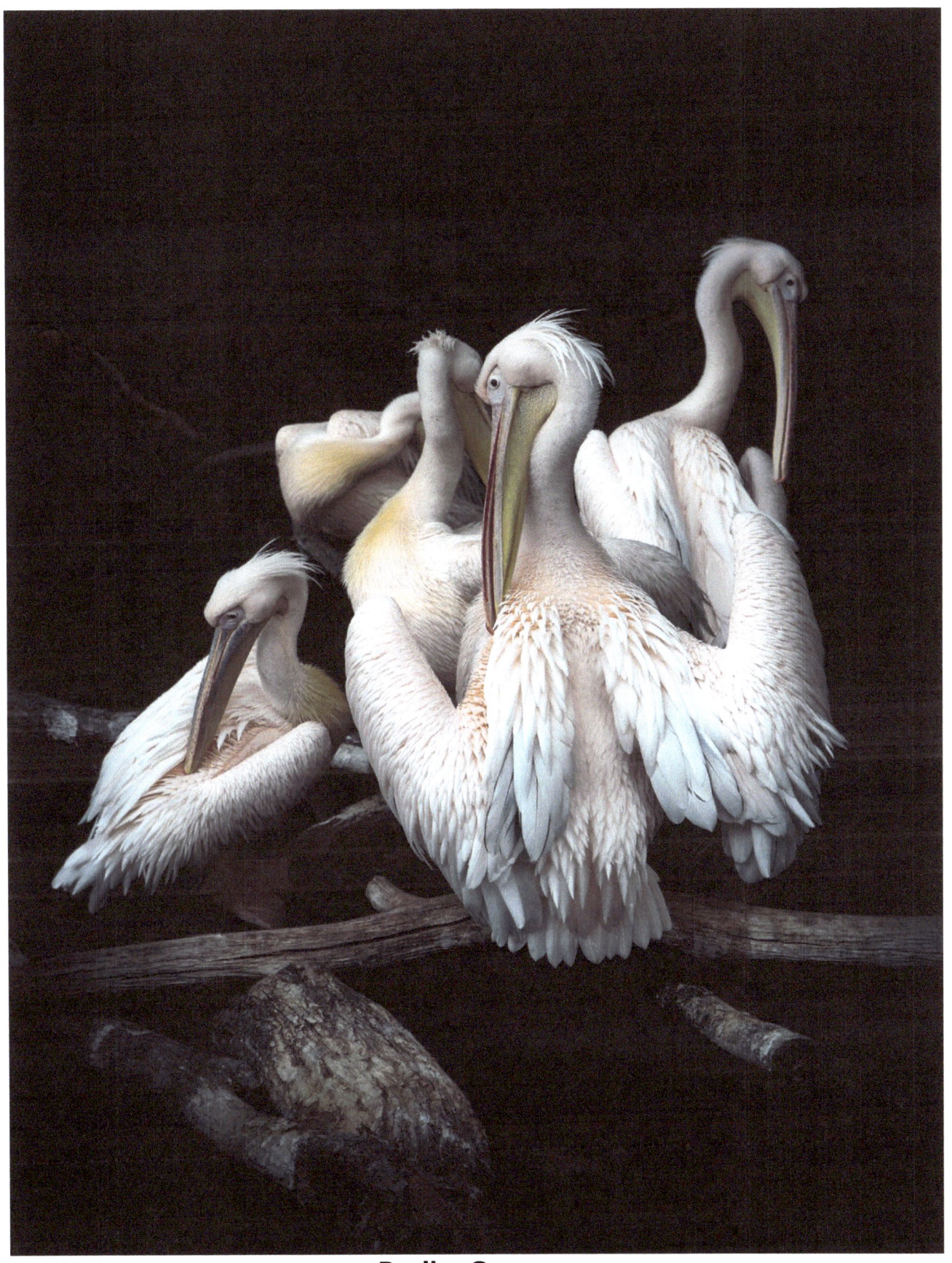

Berlin, Germany
Photographer: Oliver Guillard – Berlin, Germany

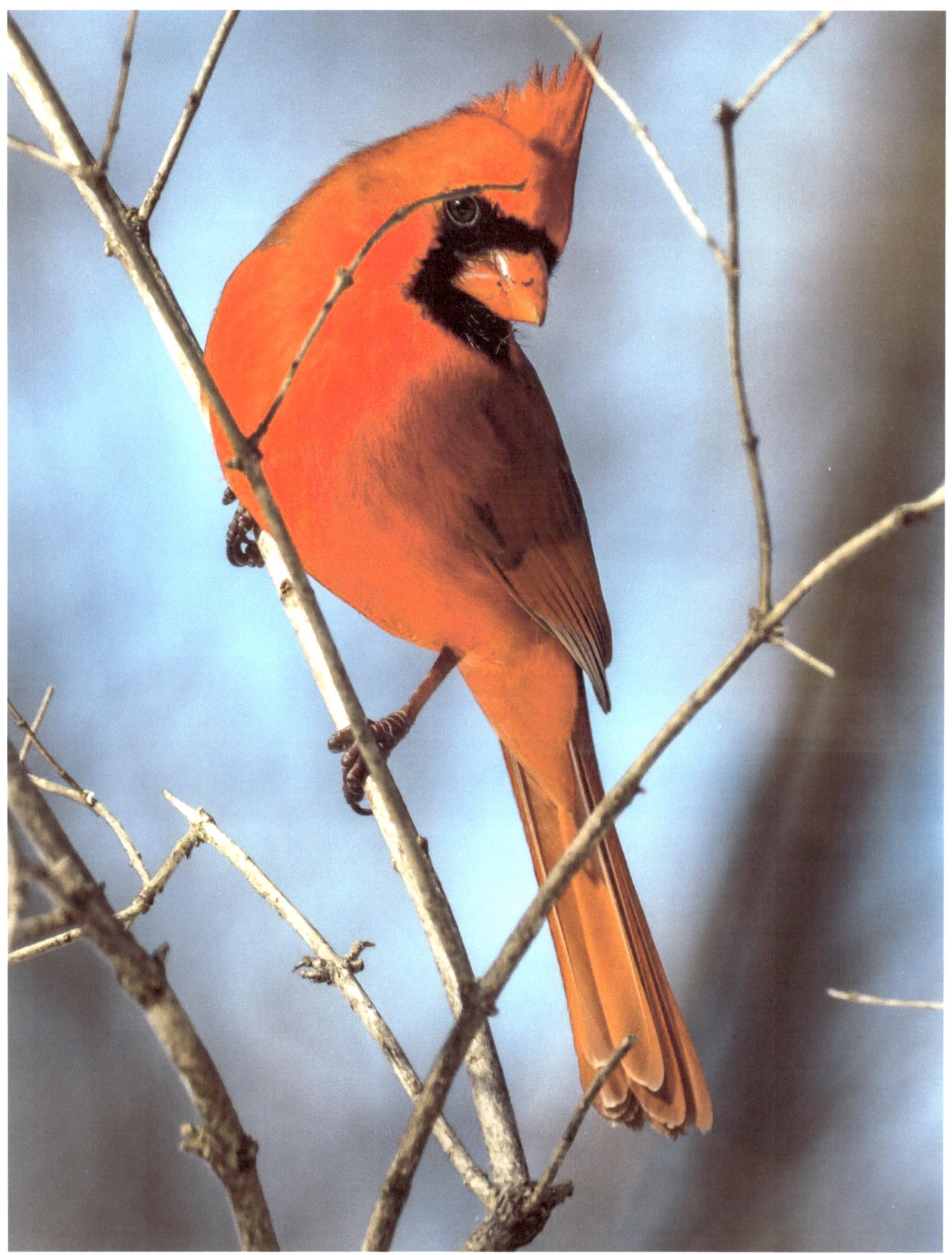

Ontario, Canada
Photographer: Patrice Bouchard – New Market, Ontario, Canada

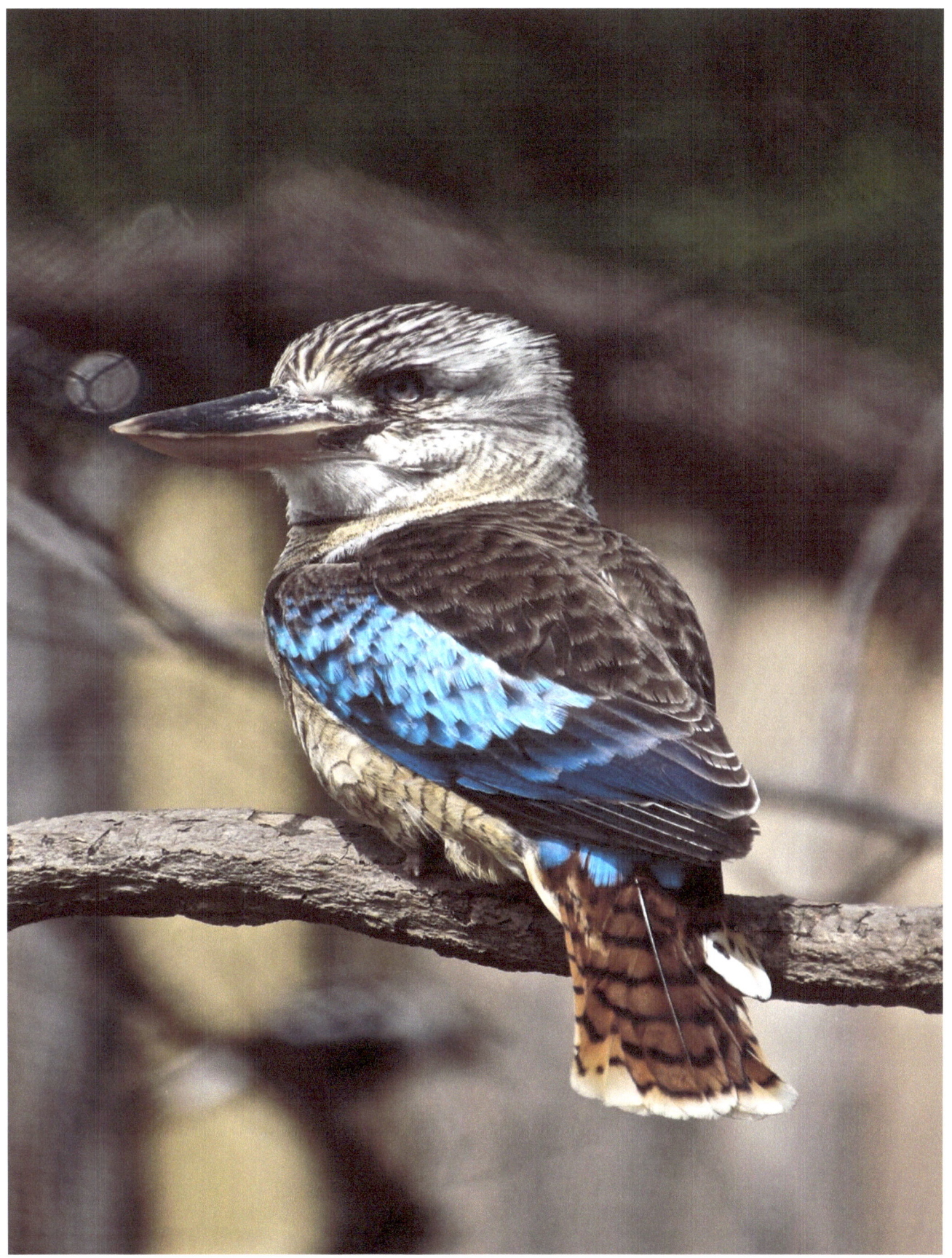

Zoo of Prague
Photographer: Peter Scholten - Netherlands

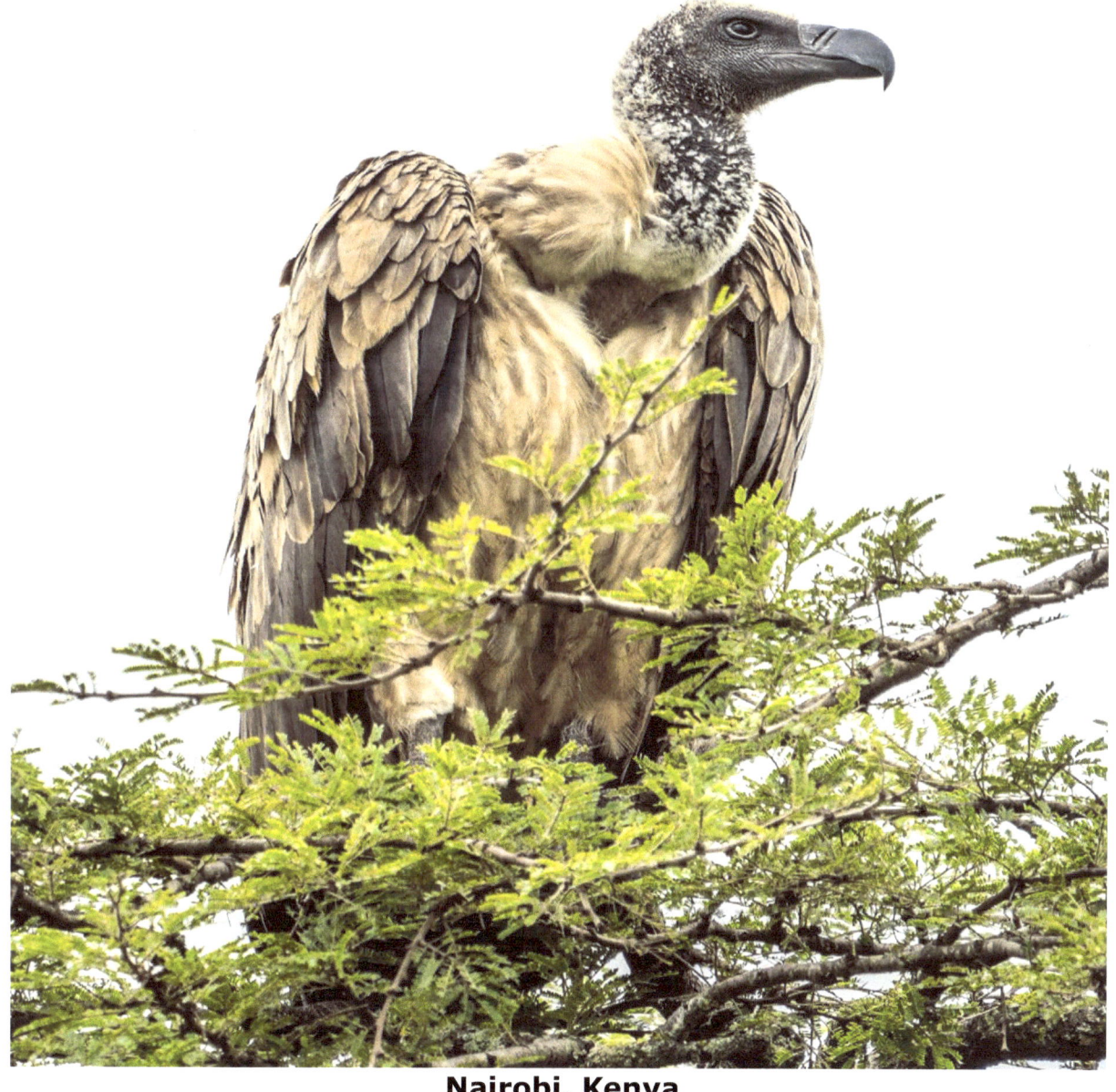

Nairobi, Kenya
Photographer: Photos by Beks - Kenya

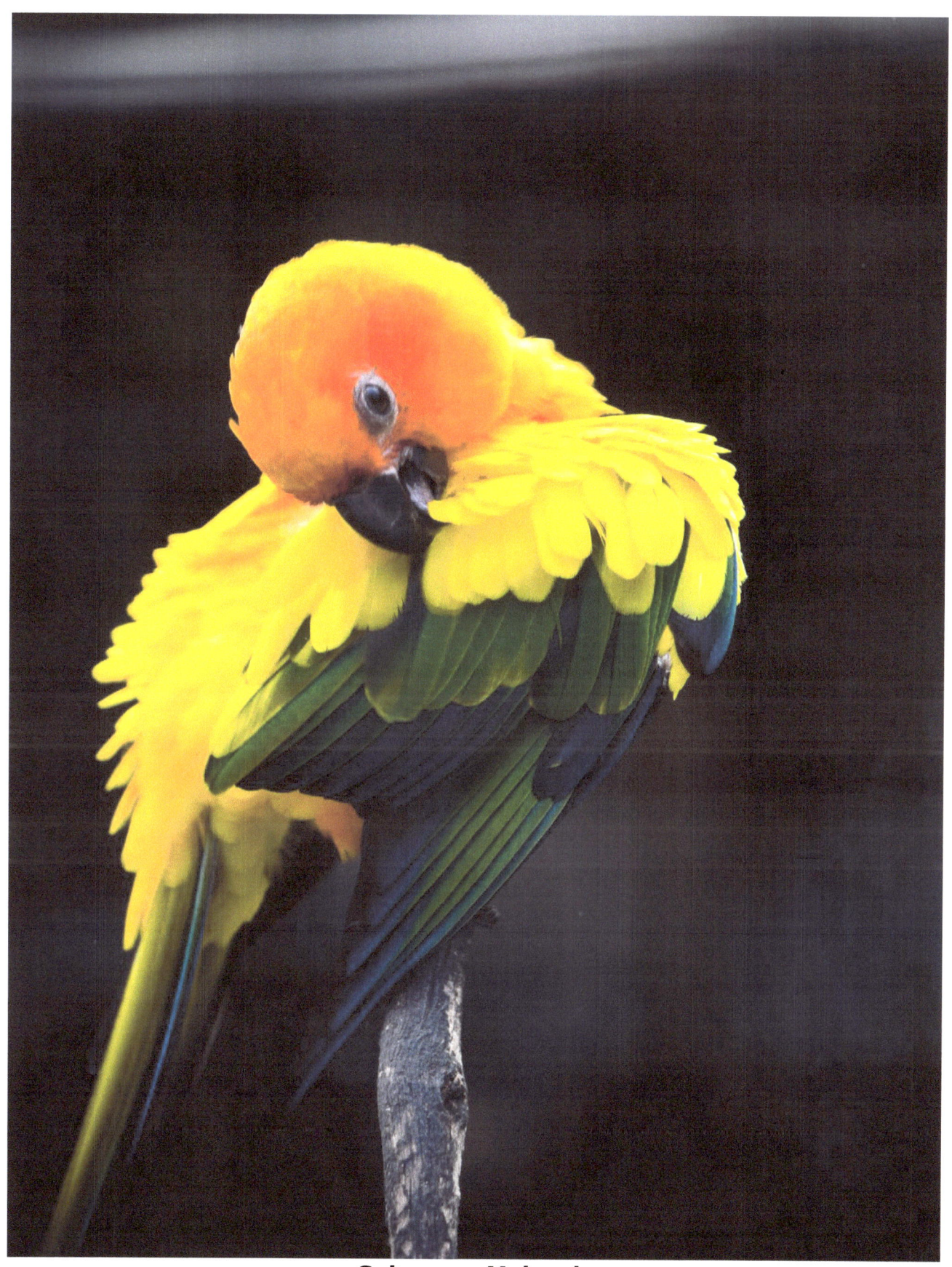

Solanger, Malaysia
Photographer: Ravin Rau

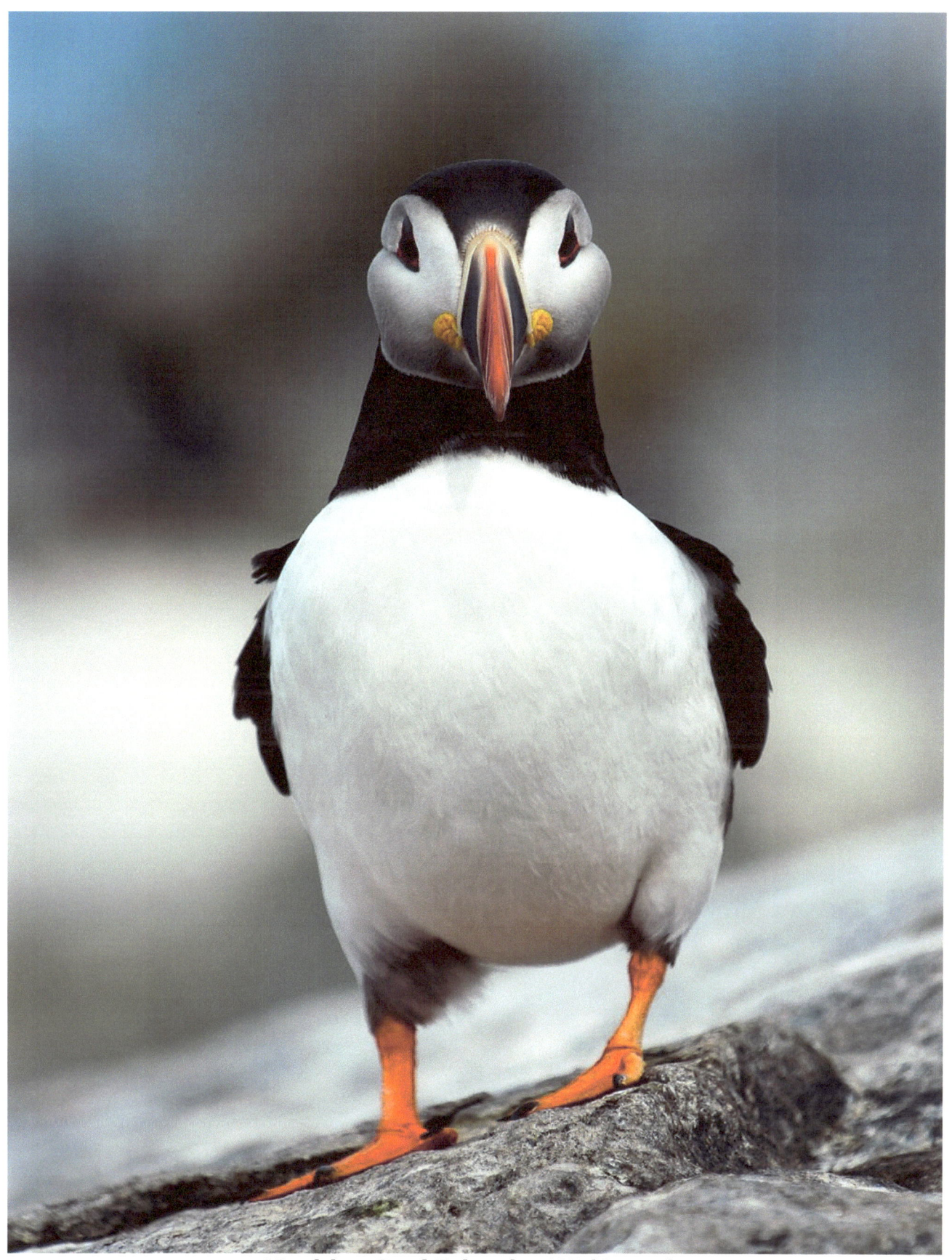

Machias Seal Island – US/Canada
Photographer: Ray Hennessy – Clementon, New Jersey

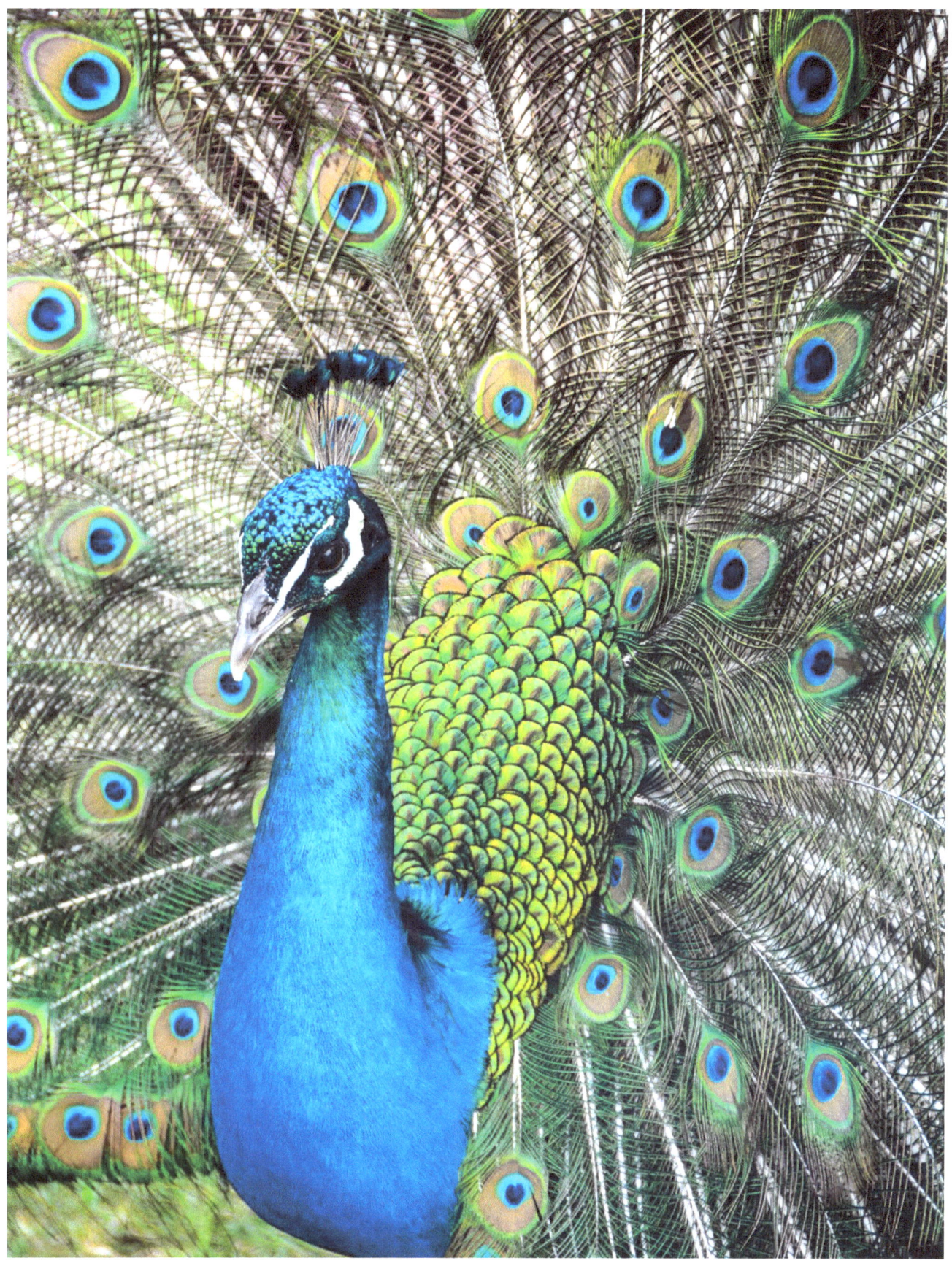

Photographer: Ricardo Frantz – Paris, France

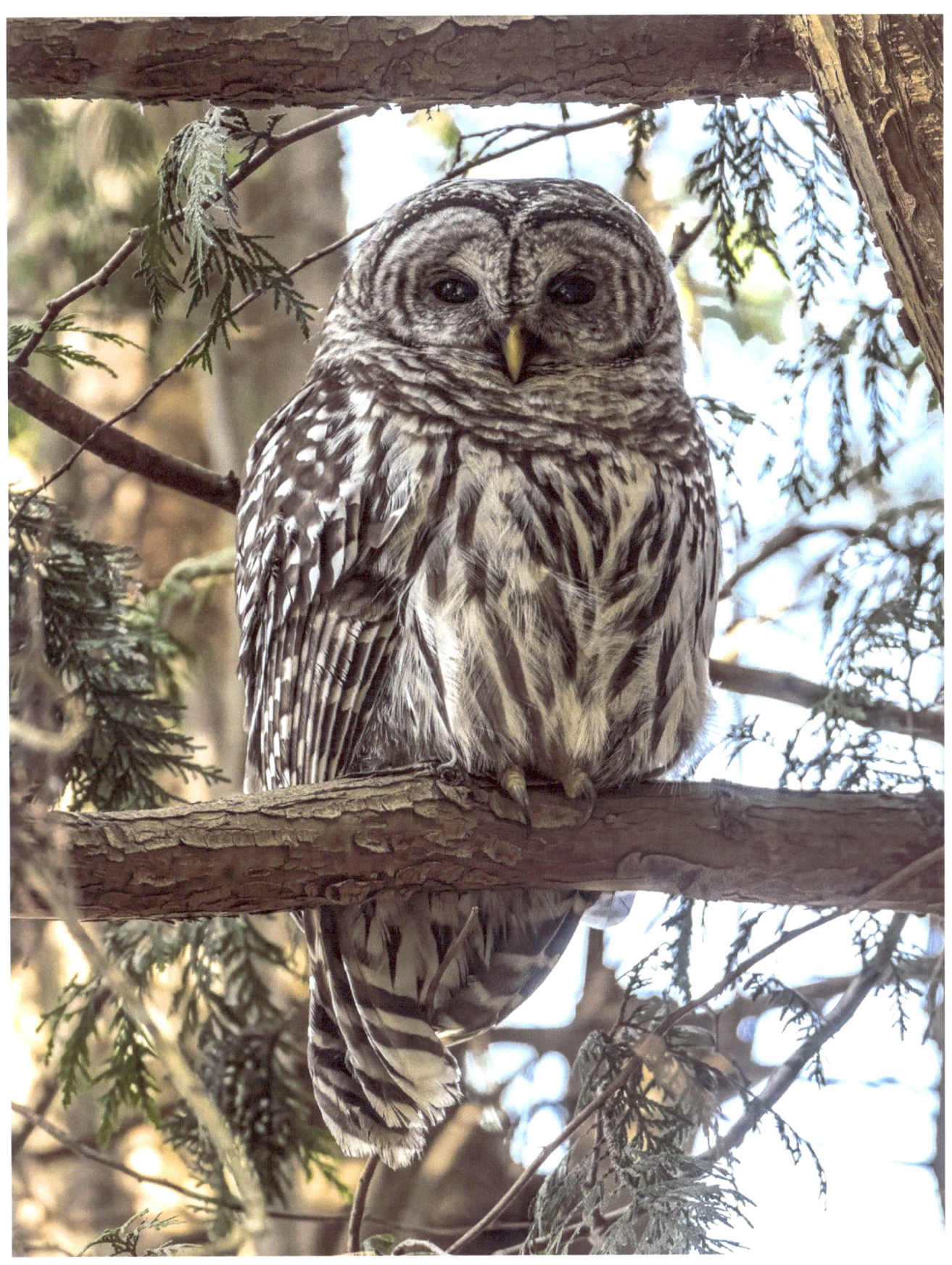

Photographer: Richard Lee – Abbotsford, British Columbia

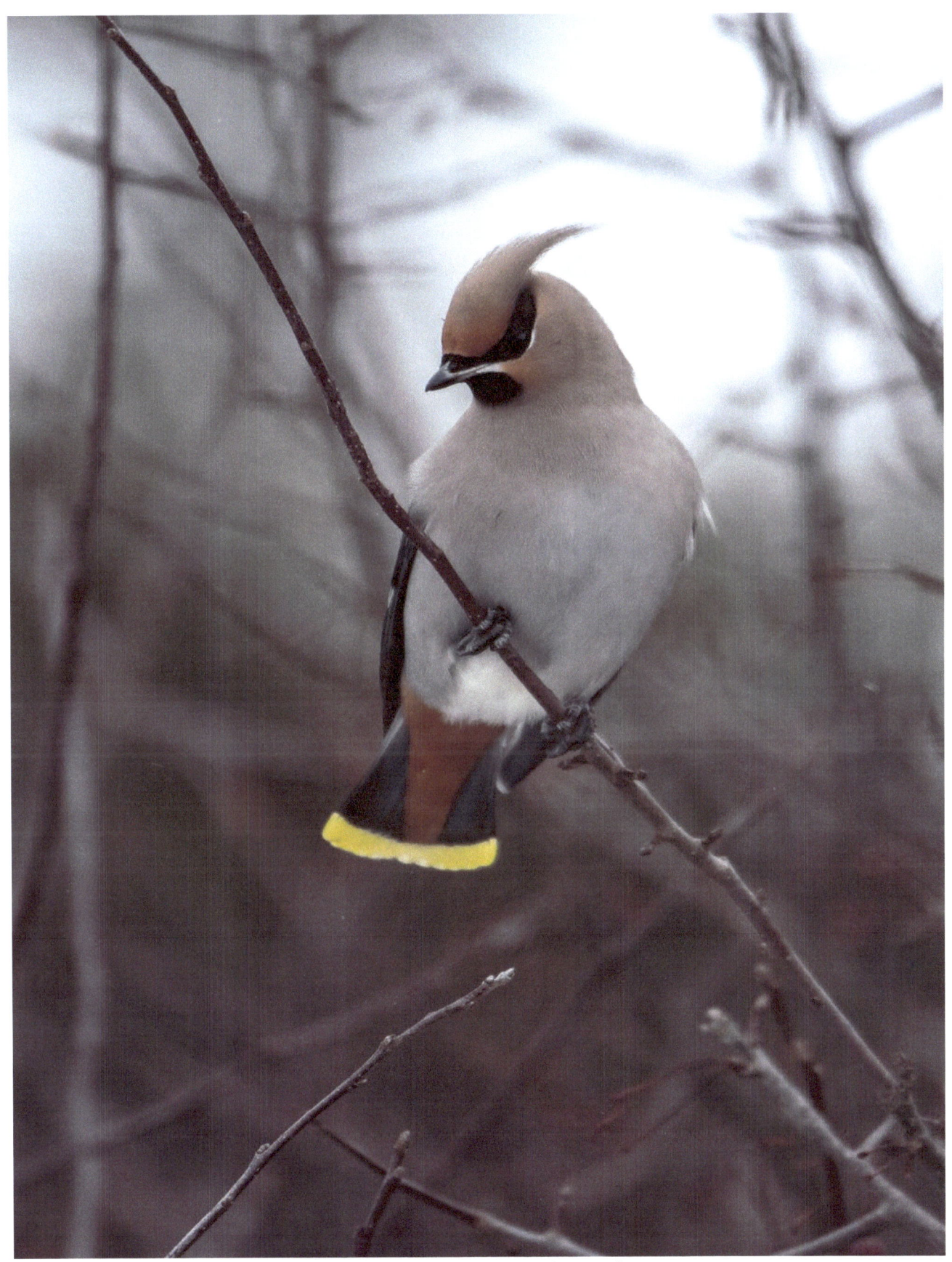

Dufferin County, Canada
Photographer: Richard Lee – Abbotsford, British Columbia

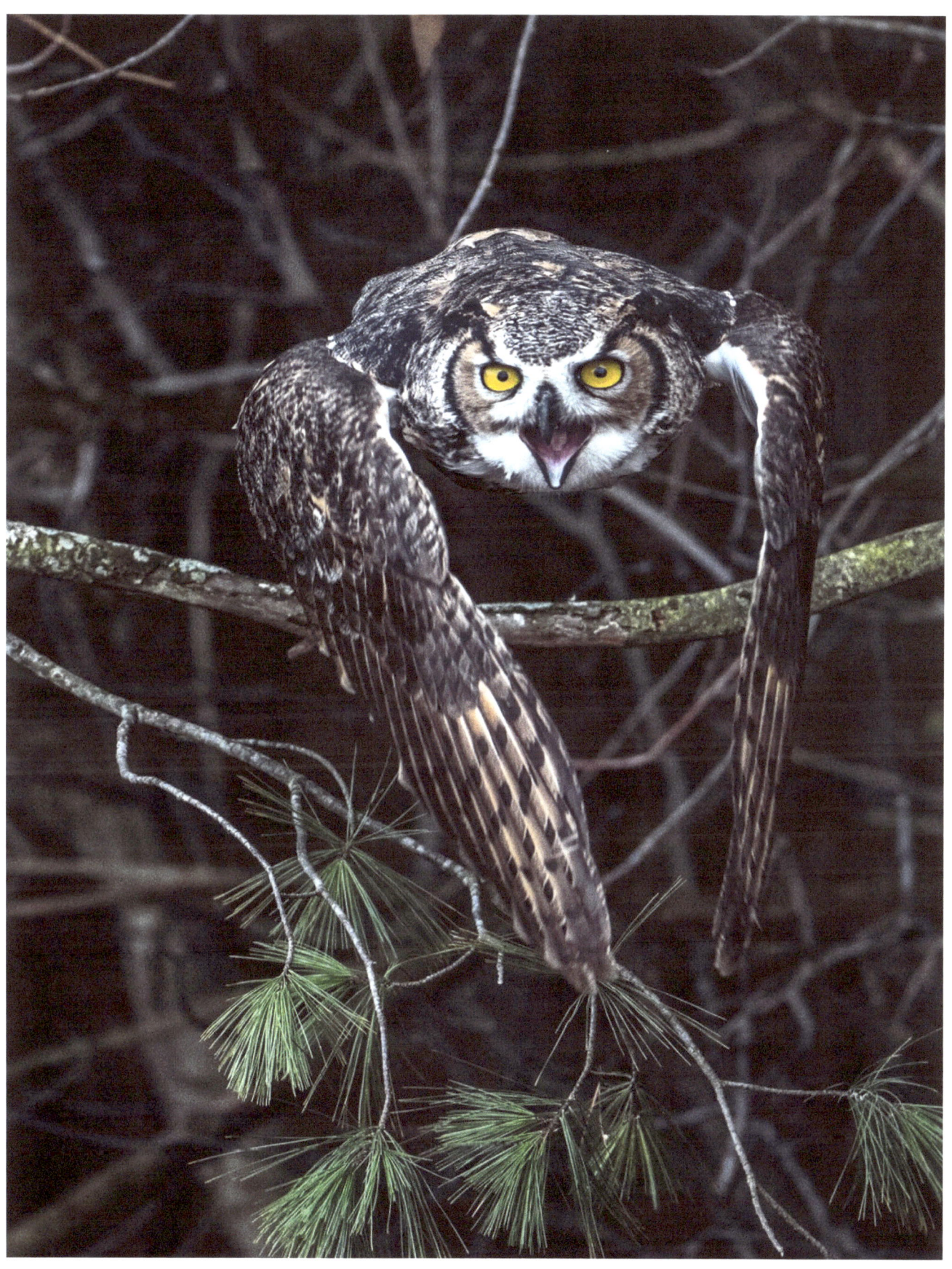

Photographer: Richard Lee – Abbotsford, British Columbia

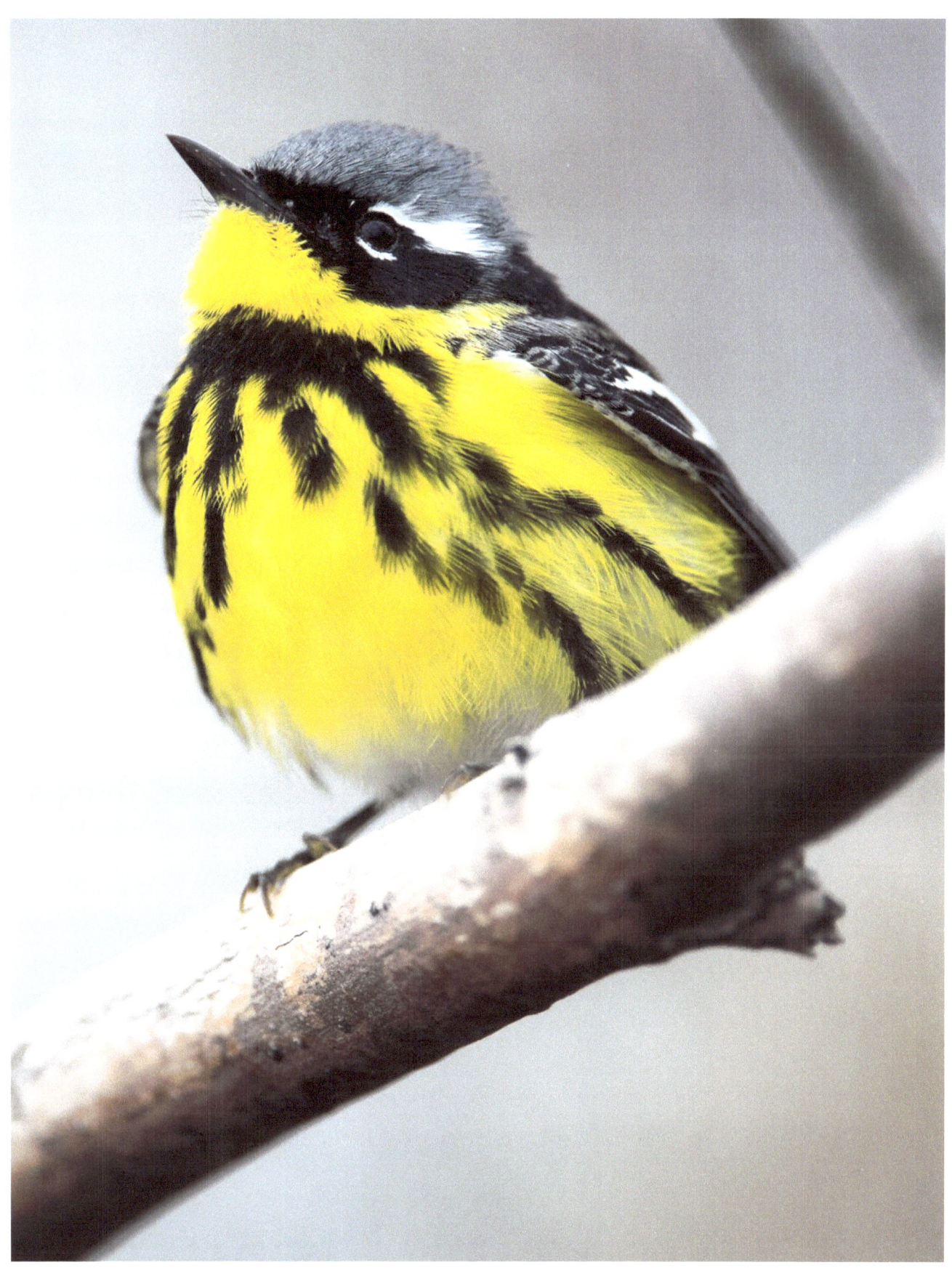

Photographer: Richard Lee – Abbotsford, British Columbia

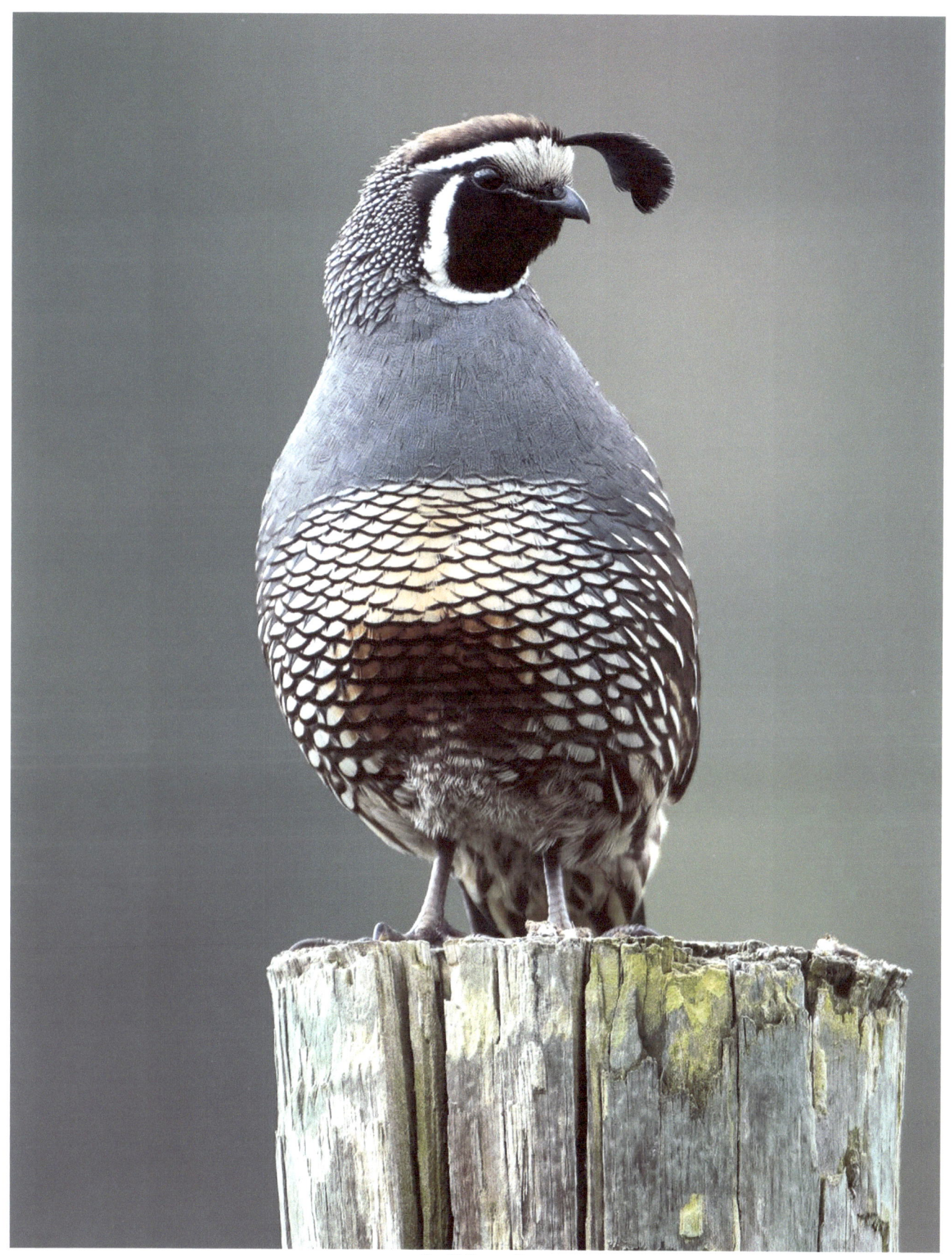

California
Photographer: Richard Lee – Abbotsford, British Columbia

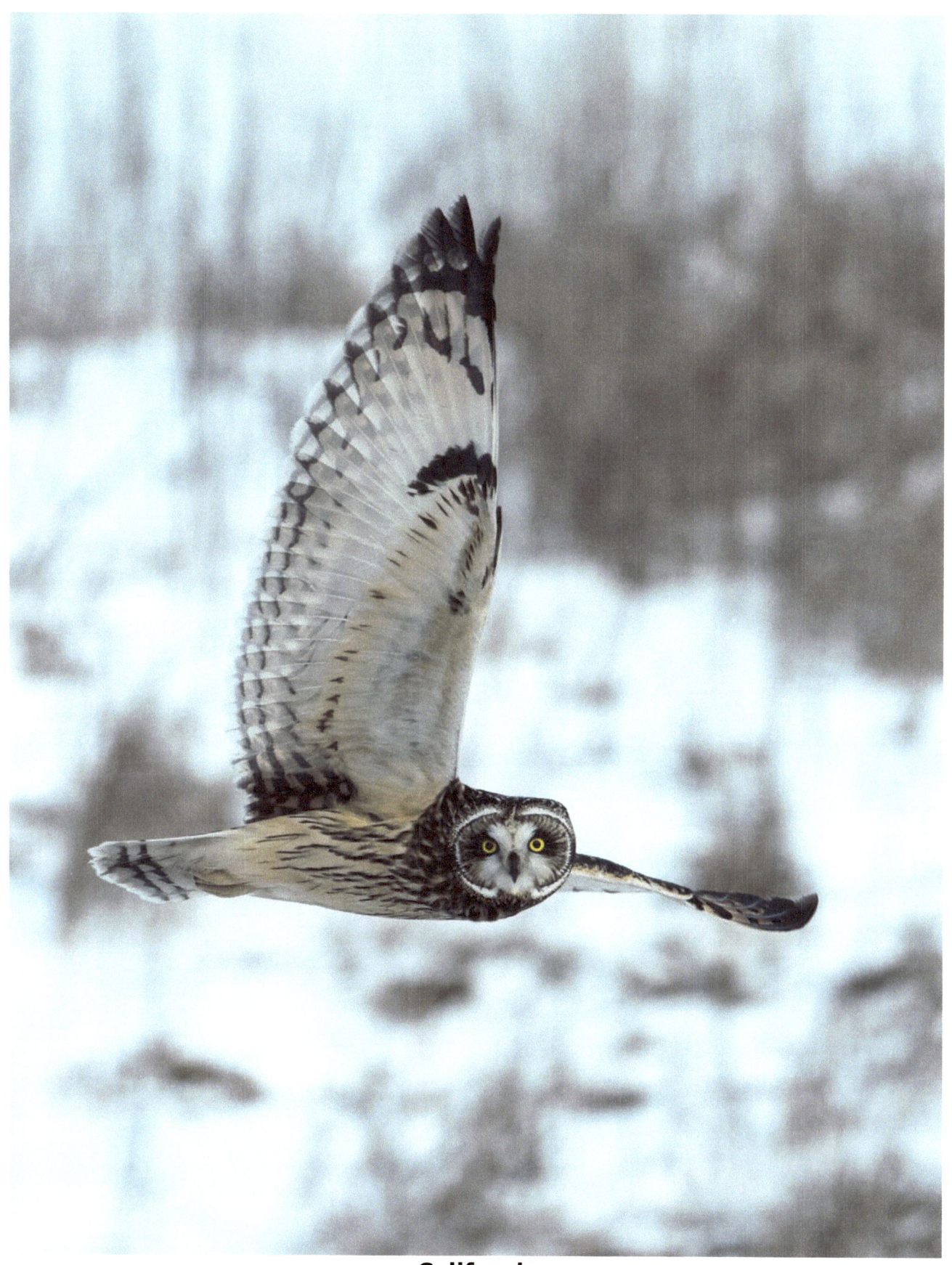

California
Photographer: Richard Lee – Abbotsford, British Columbia

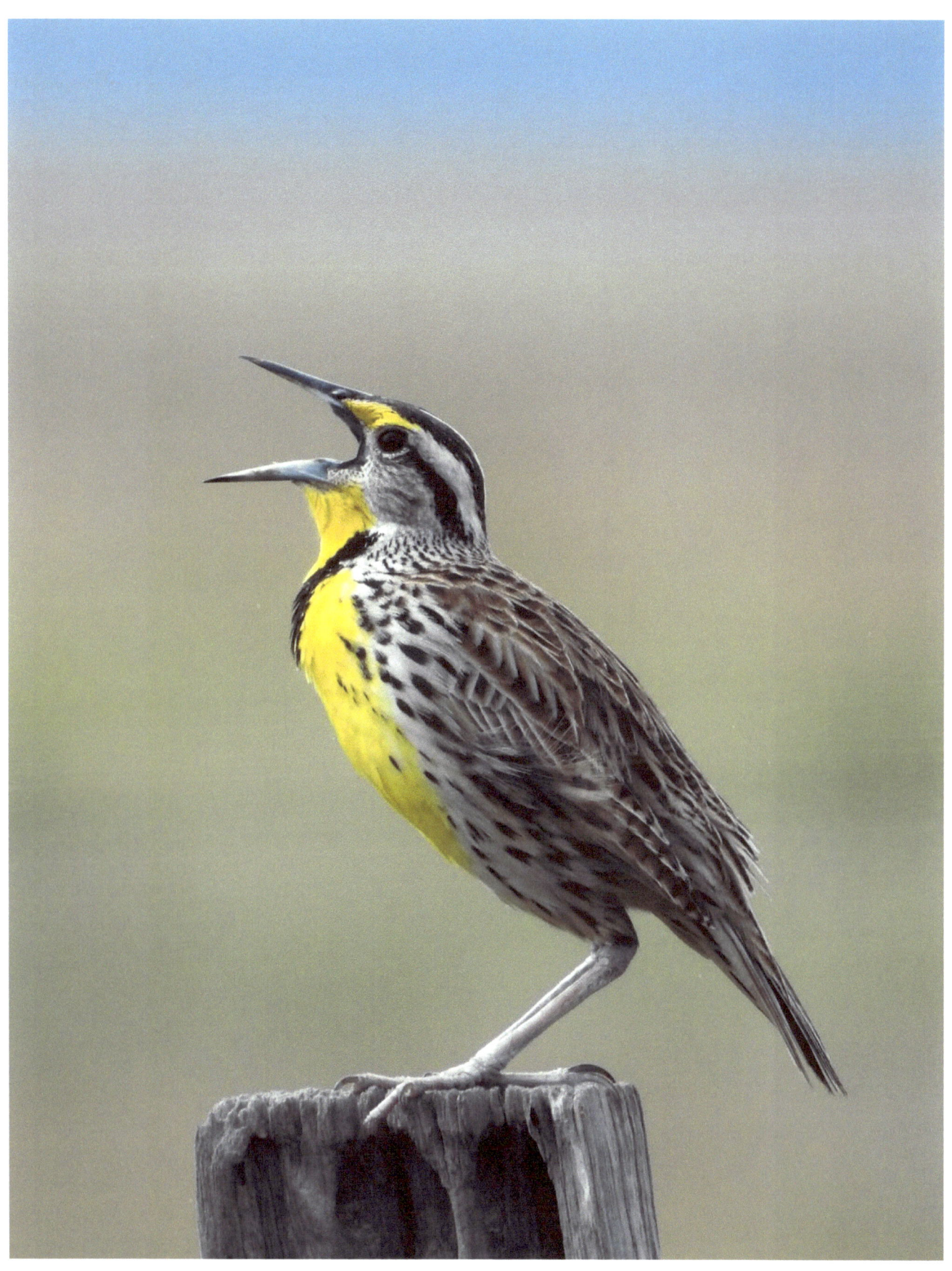

Photographer: Rogean James Caleffi – Roraima, Venezuala

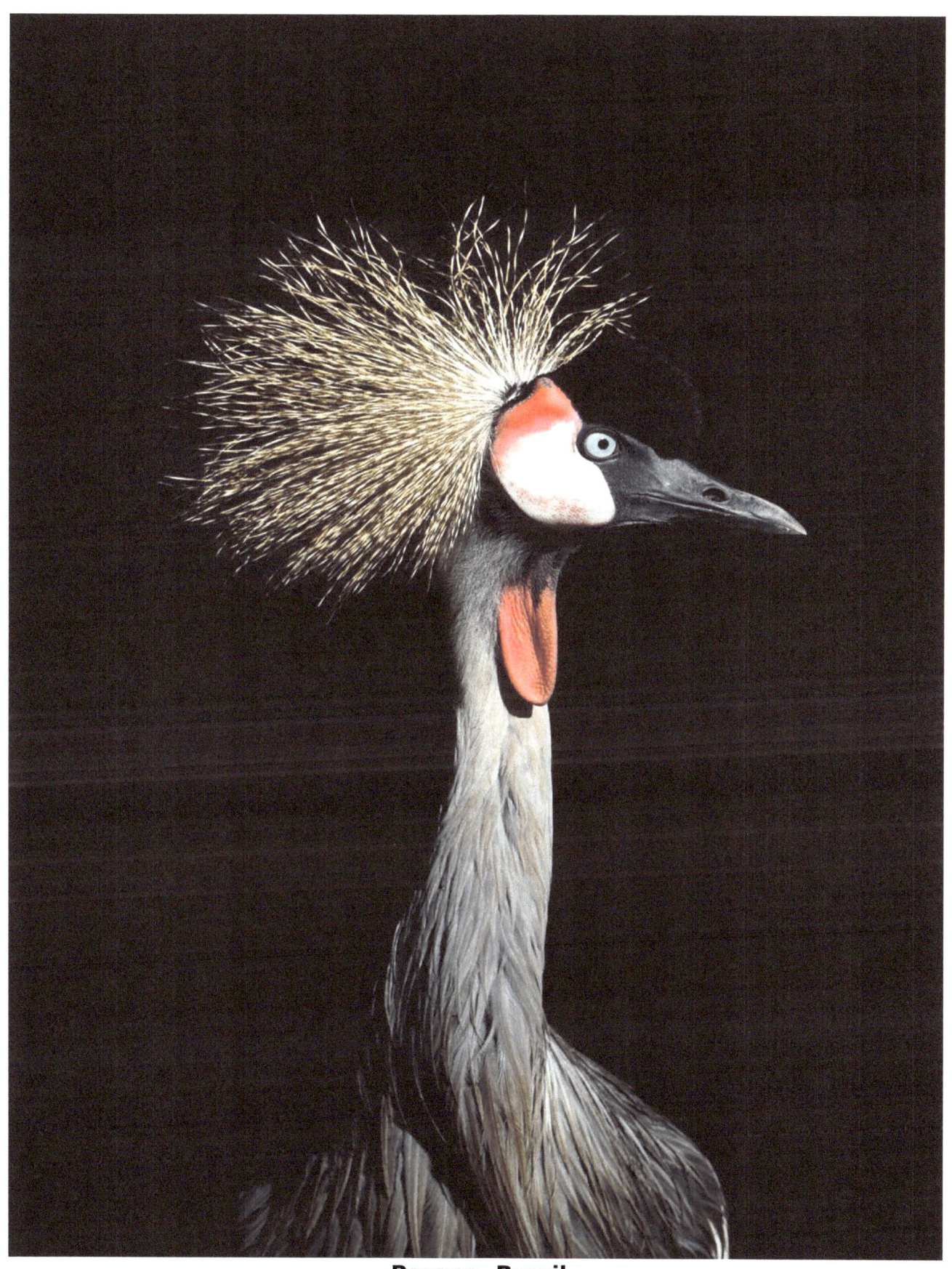

Parana, Brazil
Photographer: Seiji Seiji

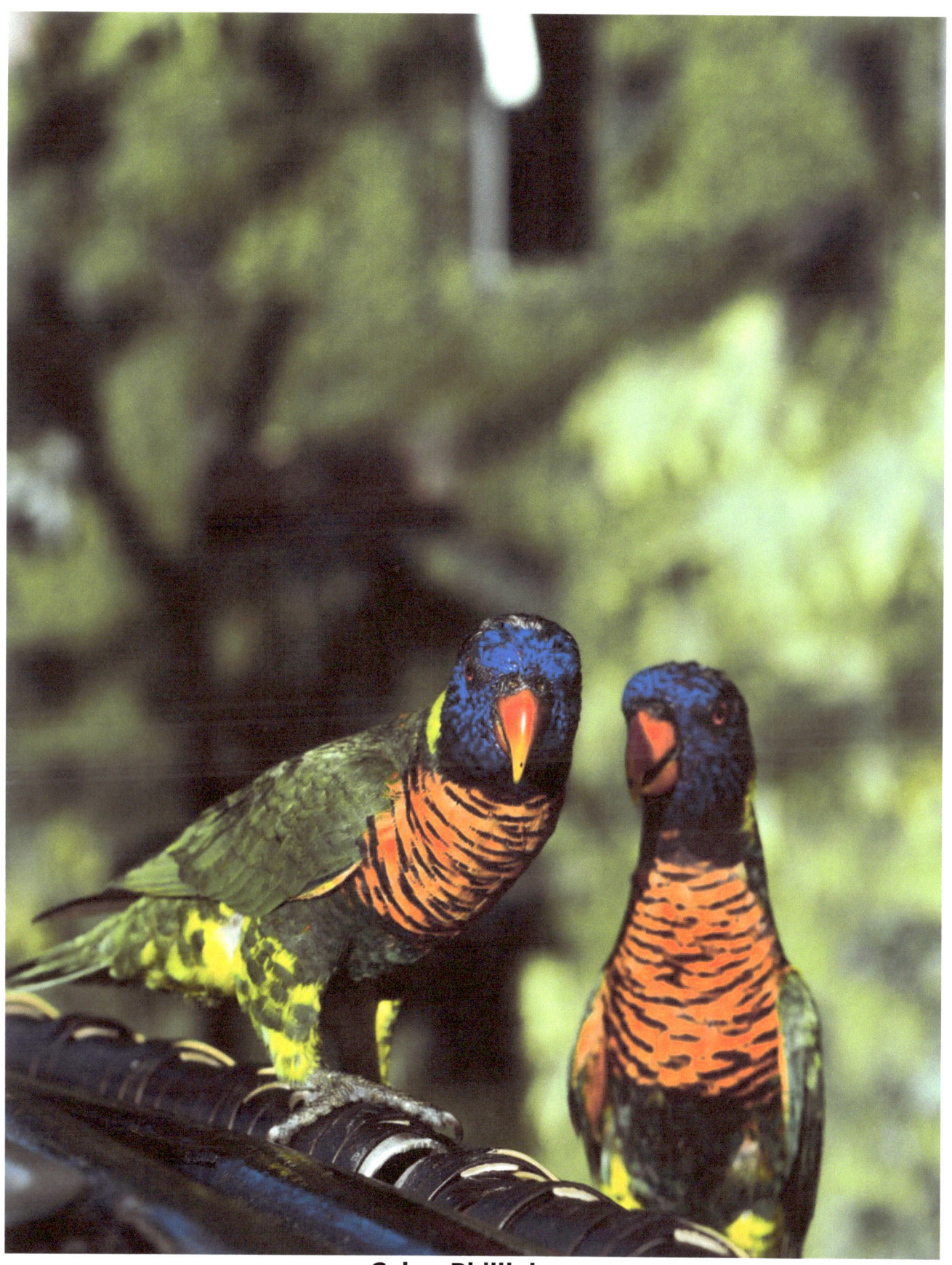

Cebu, Phillipines
Photographer: Shaira Torlao

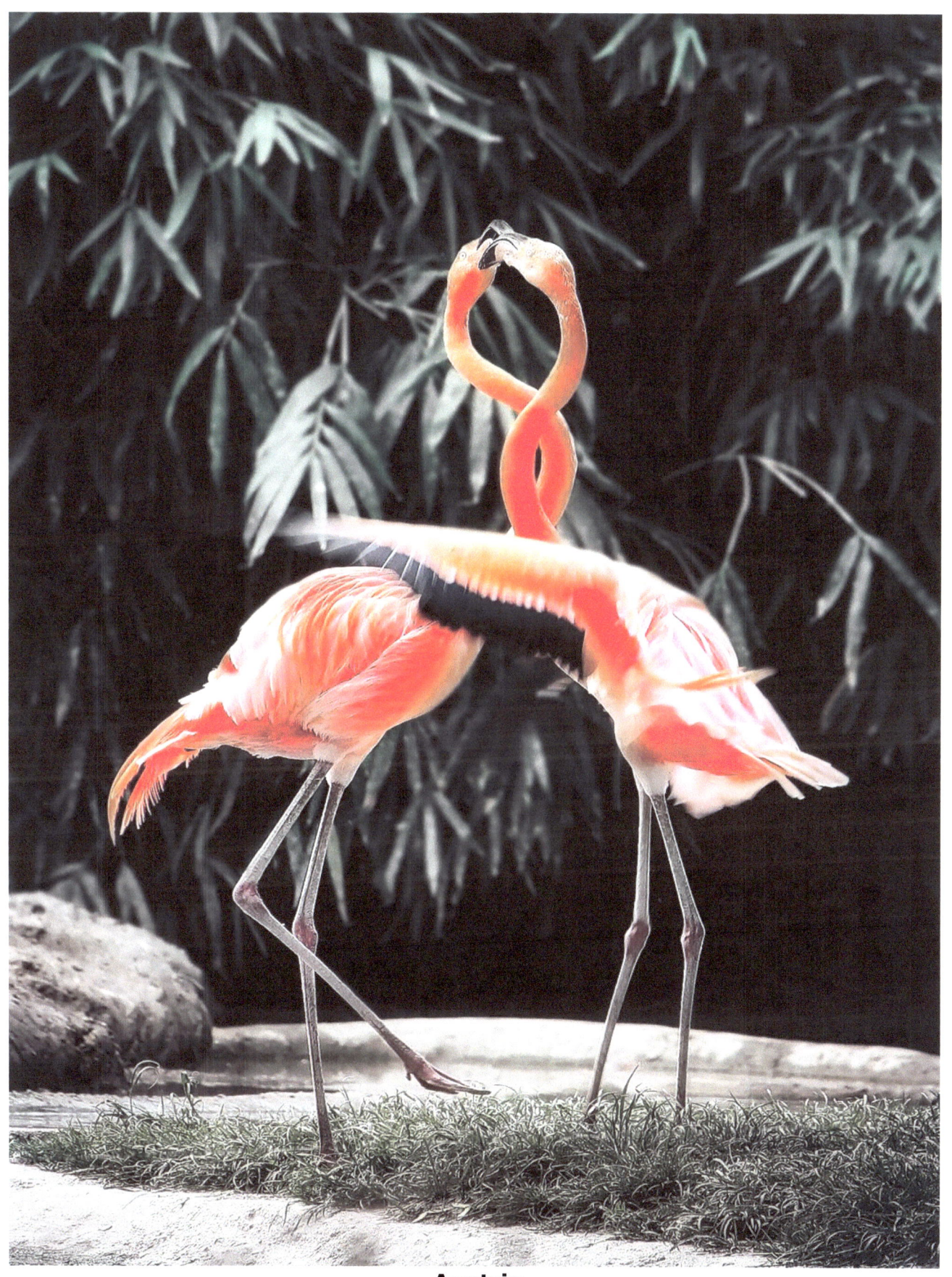

Austria
Photographer: Simon Berger - Austria

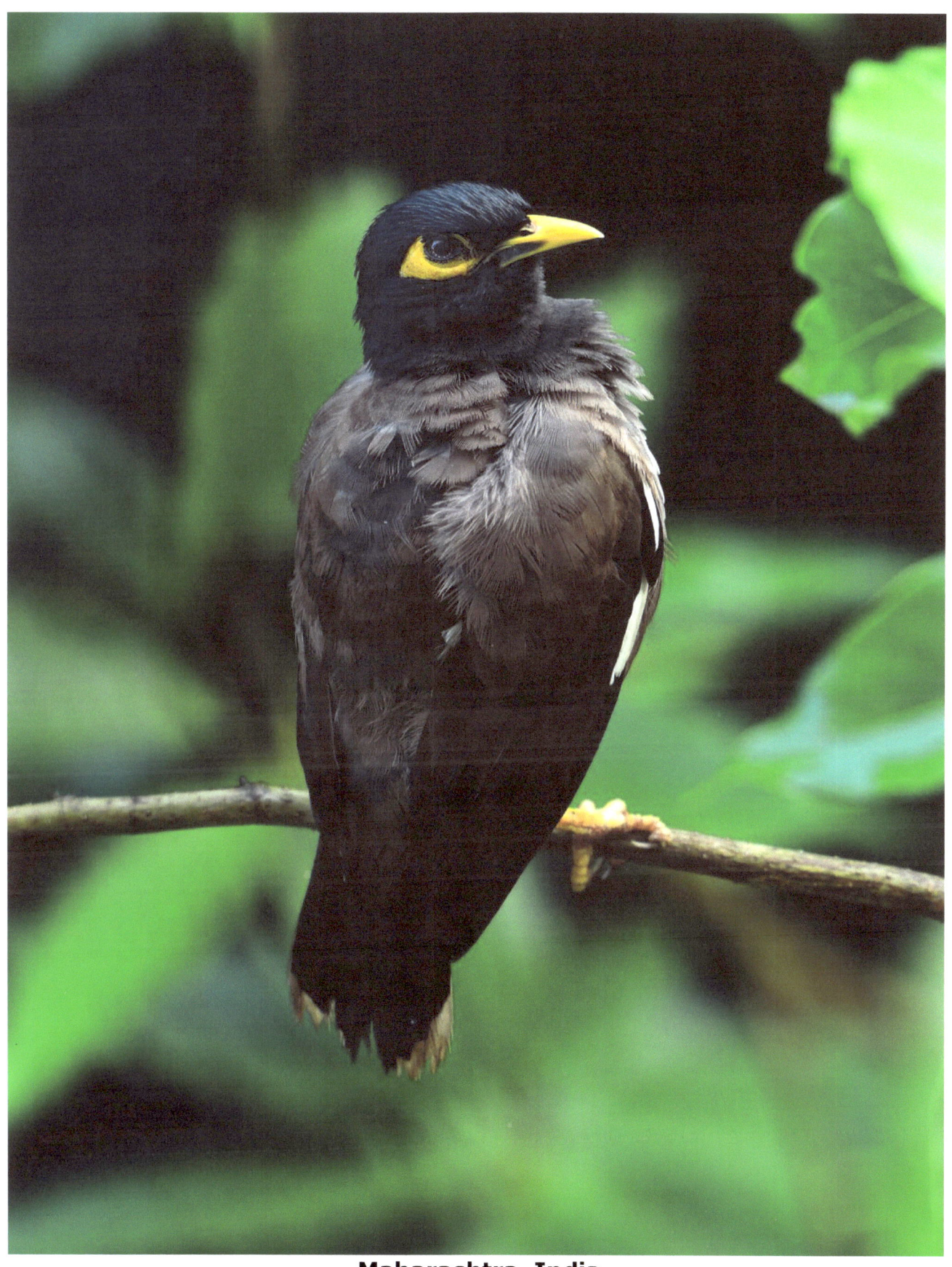

Maharashtra, India
Photographer: Sreenivas - India

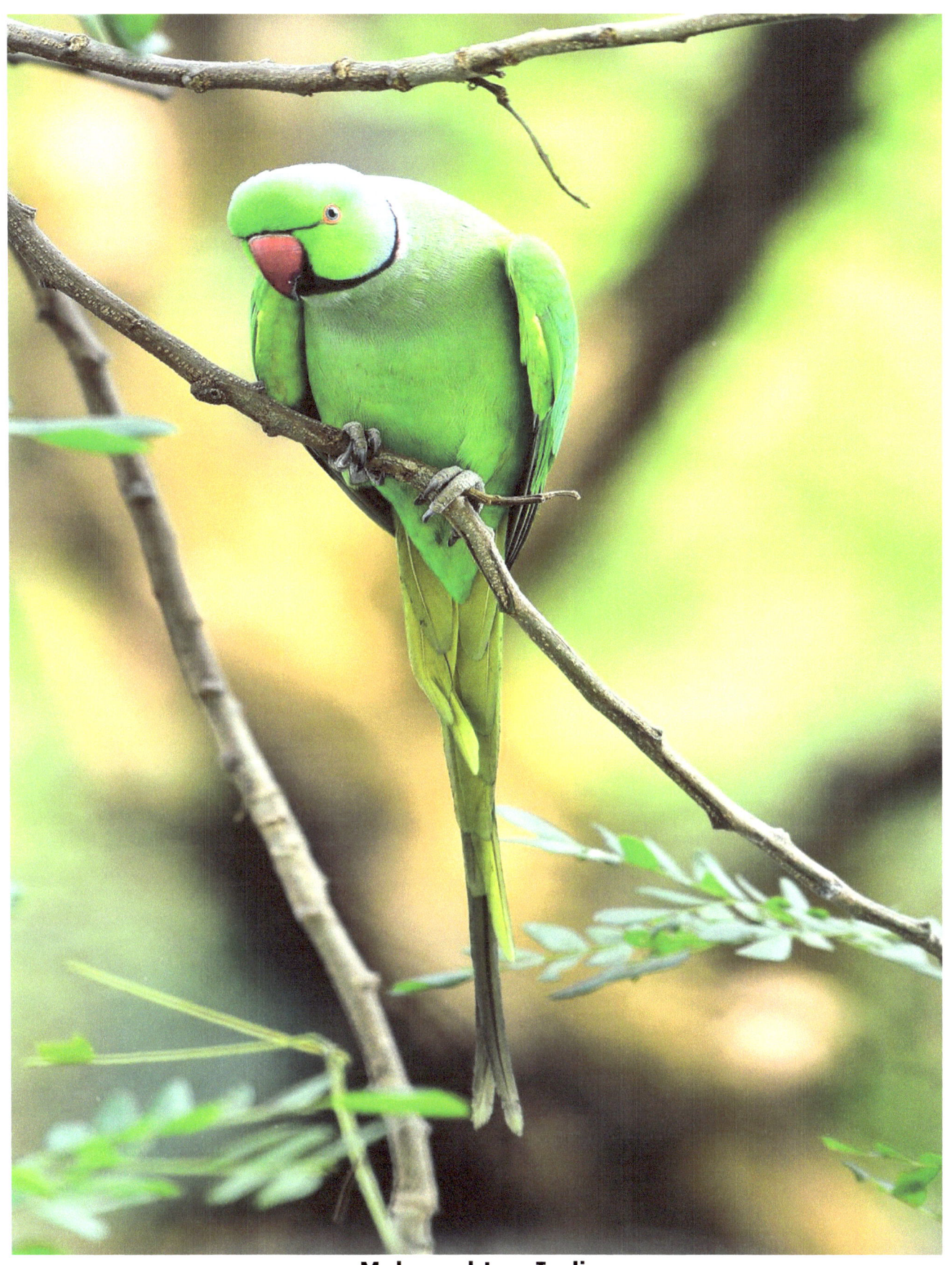

Maharashtra, India
Photographer: Sreenivas - India

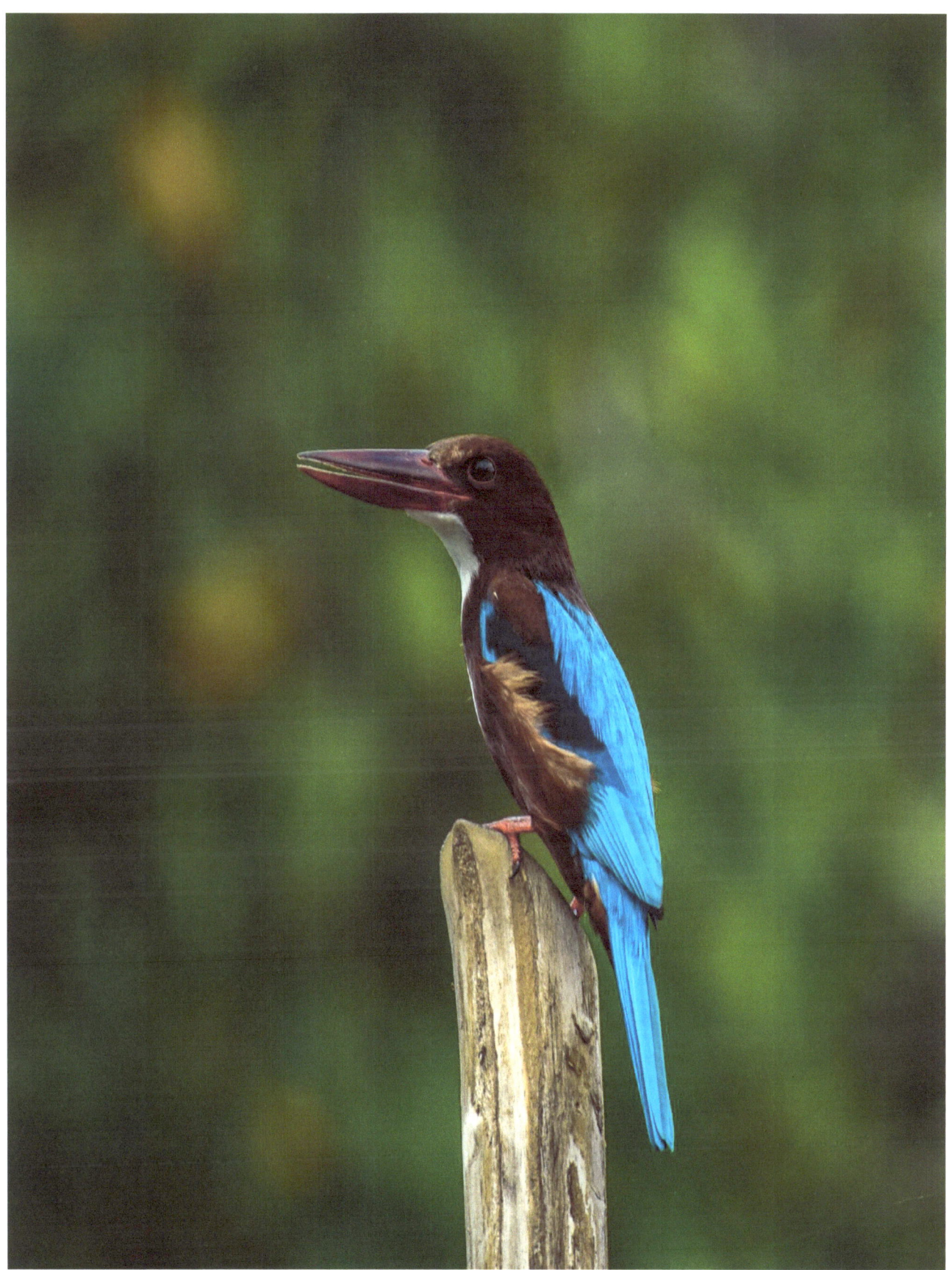

Sri Lanka
Photographer: Thomas Maximillian Lener - Austria

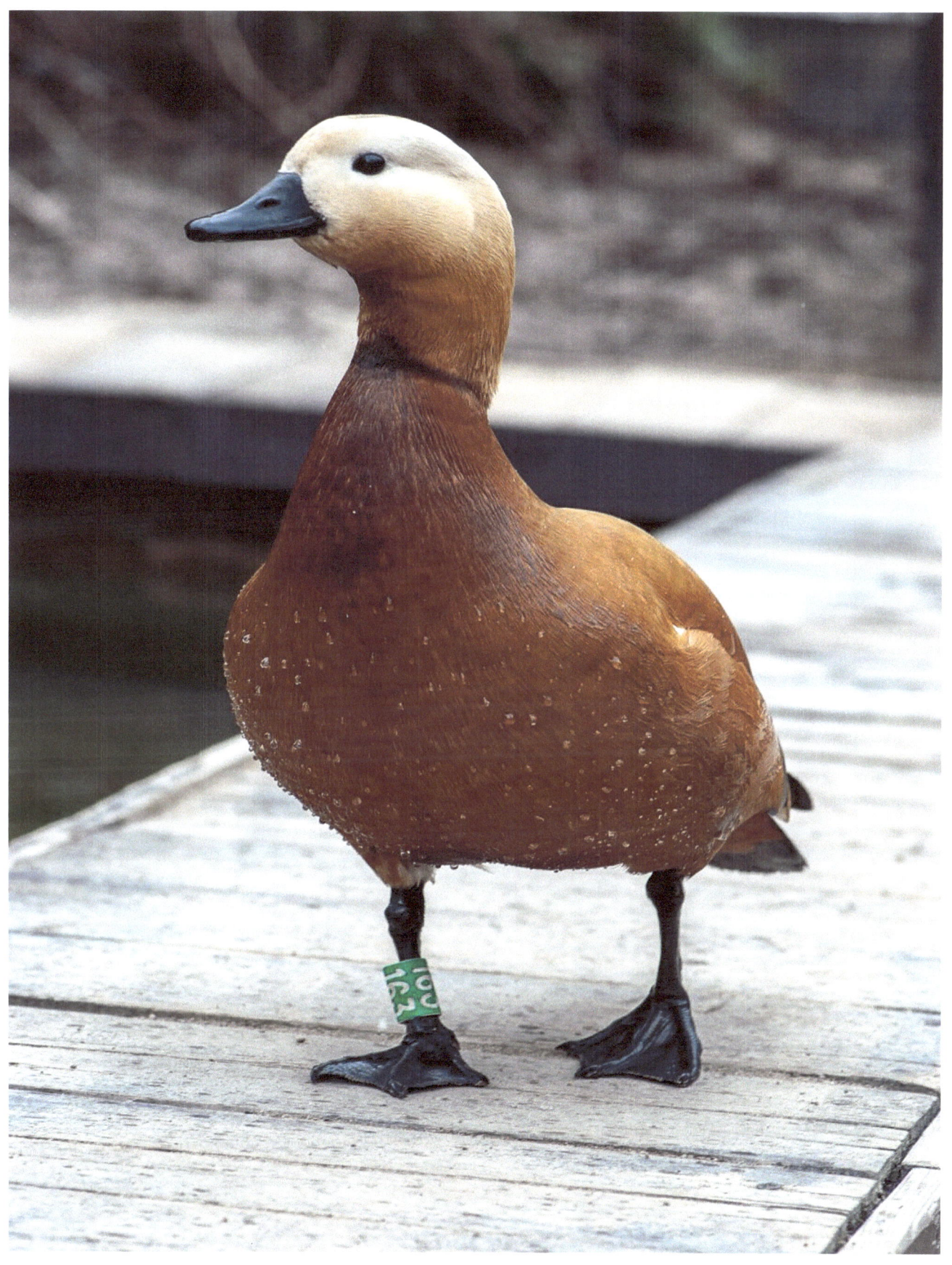

Photographer: Yoksel Zok – Moscow, Russia

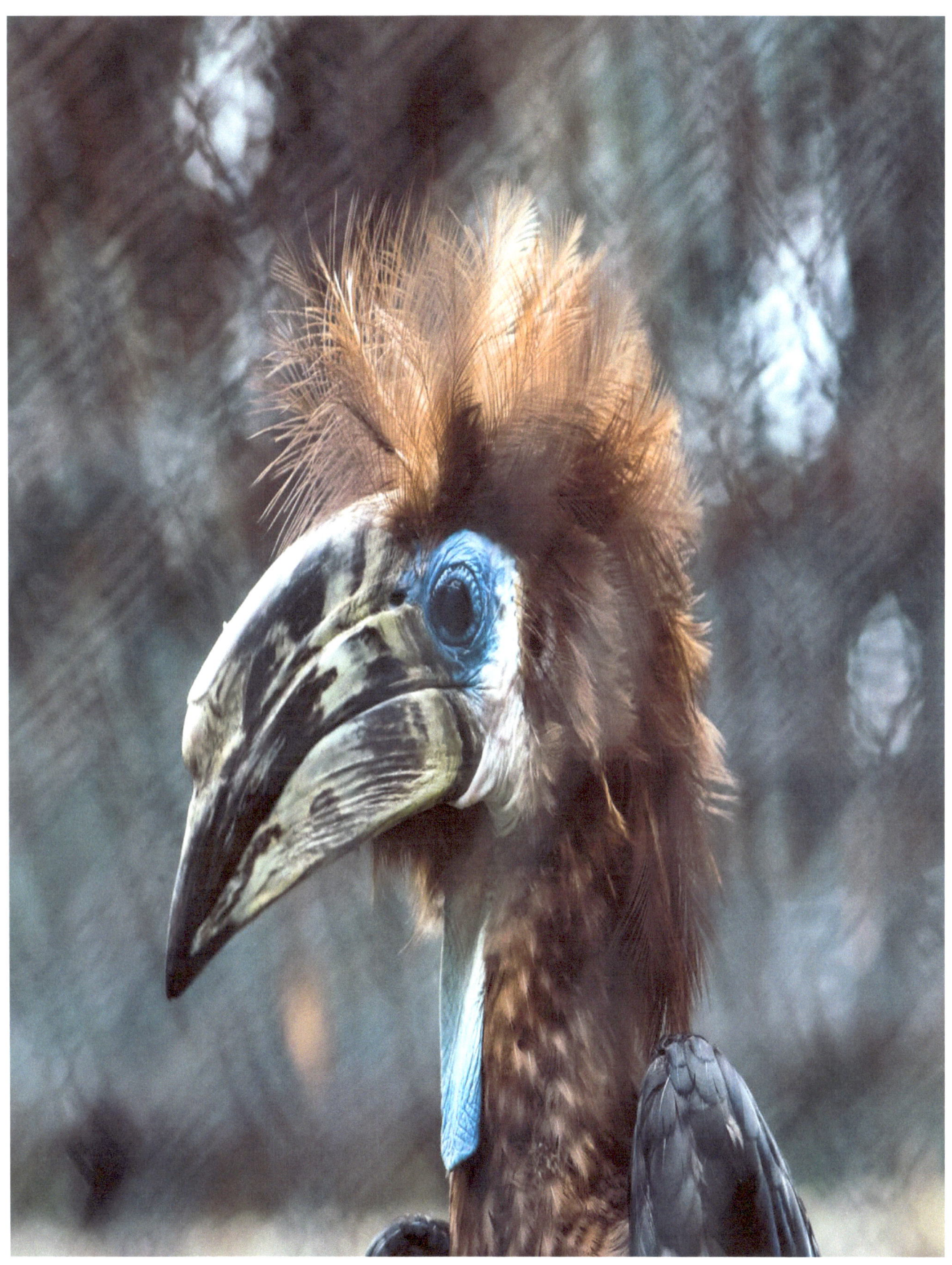

Photographer: Tomas Vydrzal

www.ingramcontent.com/pod-product-compliance
Lightning Source LLC
Chambersburg PA
CBHW041930240526
45473CB00034B/721